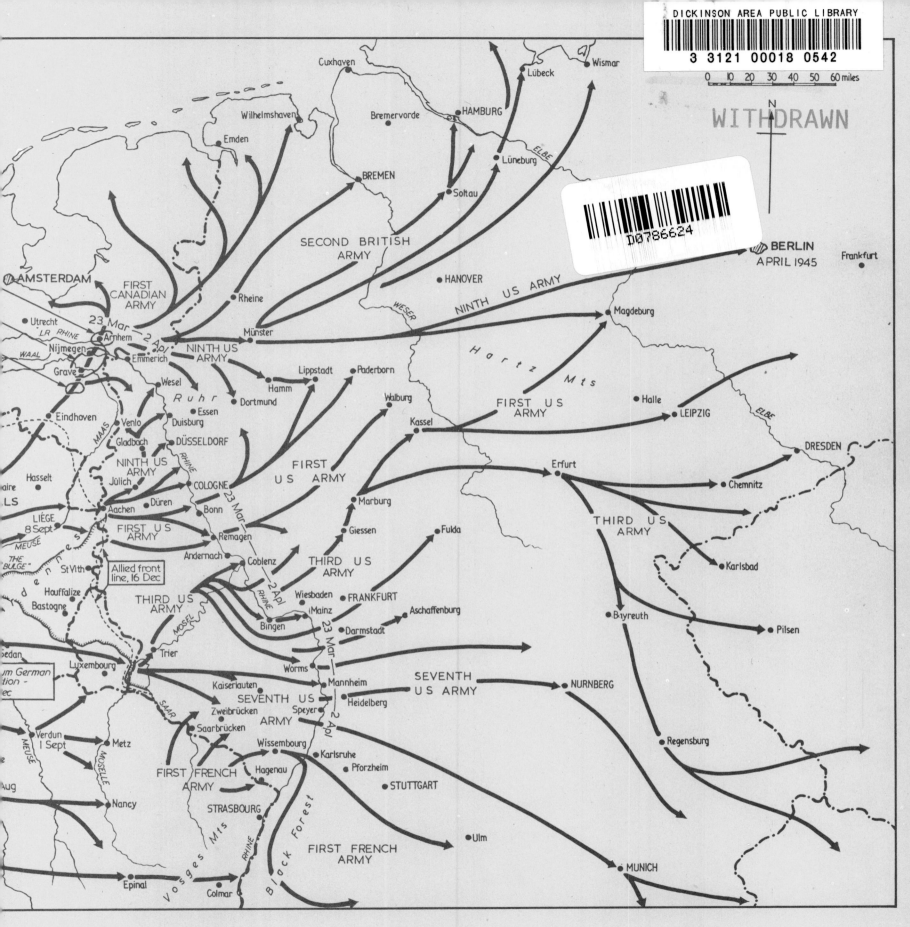

0 10 20 30 40 50 60 miles

N

Cuxhaven

Wismar

Lübeck

HAMBURG

Wilhelmshaven

Bremervorde

Lüneburg

Emden

BREMEN

ELBE

Soltau

SECOND BRITISH
ARMY

BERLIN
APRIL 1945

Frankfurt

AMSTERDAM

HANOVER

NINTH US ARMY

FIRST
CANADIAN
ARMY

Rheine

WESER

Utrecht

23 Mar

Magdeburg

LR. RHINE

Arnhem

2 Apl

Münster

Nijmegen

WAAL

Emmerich

NINTH US
ARMY

Hartz   Mts

Grave

Wesel

Lippstadt

Paderborn

FIRST US
ARMY

Halle

LEIPZIG

Ruhr

Hamm

Dortmund

Walburg

ELBE

Eindhoven

Essen

Kassel

DRESDEN

Venlo

Duisburg

Gladbach

DÜSSELDORF

aire

Hasselt

RHINE

NINTH US
ARMY

Jülich

COLOGNE

FIRST
US ARMY

Erfurt

Chemnitz

LS

Aachen

Düren

Marburg

LIÉGE
8 Sept

Bonn

23 Mar

THIRD US
ARMY

MEUSE

FIRST US
ARMY

Remagen

Giessen

Fulda

Karlsbad

THE
BULGE

St Vith

Andernach

Coblenz

2 Apl

Bayreuth

Hauffalize

THIRD US
ARMY

RHINE

Wiesbaden

FRANKFURT

Pilsen

Bastogne

Mainz

Aschaffenburg

MOSEL

Sedan

Trier

Bingen

23 Mar

Darmstadt

um German
tion -
ec

Luxembourg

Worms

2 Apl

SEVENTH
US ARMY

NURNBERG

Kaiserlauten

Mannheim

SEVENTH US

Verdun
I Sept

SAAR

Zweibrücken

Speyer

Heidelberg

Metz

Saarbrücken

ARMY

Regensburg

MEUSE

MOSELLE

FIRST FRENCH
ARMY

Wissembourg

Karlsruhe

Aug

Hagenau

Pforzheim

Nancy

STUTTGART

STRASBOURG

Black Forest

FIRST FRENCH
ARMY

Ulm

Vosges Mts

RHINE

MUNICH

Epinal

Colmar

Allied front
line, 16 Dec

THE WAY
WE WERE

THE WAY
WE WERE

KEN BELL

UNIVERSITY OF TORONTO PRESS
Toronto Buffalo London

FURTHER READING

© University of Toronto Press 1988
Toronto Buffalo London
Printed in Italy

ISBN 0-8020-3990-1

Canadian Cataloguing in Publication Data

Bell, Ken, 1914-
  The way we were

  Bibliography: p.
  ISBN 0-8020-3990-1

  1. World War, 1939-1945 – Campaigns – Western –
  Pictorial works.   2. World War, 1939-1945 – Canada –
  Pictorial works.   I. Title.

D743.2.B44 1988   940.54'0971   C88-094030-1

Byers, A.R., ed. *The Canadians at War, 1939–1945*. Montreal:
  The Reader's Digest Association (Canada), 1986
Denis, W., and Shelagh Whitaker. *Tug of War*. Toronto: Stoddart,
  1984
Granatstein, J.L., and Desmond Morton. *Bloody Victory*. Toronto:
  Lester & Orpen Dennys, 1984
Hunter, T. Murray. *Canada at Dieppe*. Ottawa: Canada War Museum
  Historical Publication No. 17, 1982
McKee, Alexander. *Caen, Anvil of Victory*. London: Pan Editions,
  1966
Munro, Ross. *Gauntlet to Overlord*. Toronto: Macmillan, 1946
Robertson, Terence. *Dieppe, the Shame and the Glory*. Boston:
  Little, Brown, 1962
Roy, Reginald H. *1944, the Canadians in Normandy*. Toronto:
  Macmillan, 1984
Ryan, Cornelius. *The Longest Day*. New York: Simon and Schuster,
  1959
Stacey, Col. C.P. *The Canadian Army, 1939–1945*. Ottawa: King's
  Printer, 1948

CONTENTS

B

World War II is for the present generations
just "history" - no longer a reality as it still is
for me and my few surviving friends who were
fighting for the freedom we are able to enjoy now.

Ken Bell is giving us in this book pictures
which bring back many good and sad memories.
I see it as a human document of what happened
in those days.

Prince of the Netherlands.

ACKNOWLEDGMENTS

Almost half a century has passed since the days when Canadians were at war in France, Sicily, Italy, Holland, Belgium, and Germany. It was a time which saw heroic men and remarkable deeds: the sacrifices at Dieppe, the landings in Normandy, the stubborn campaign in Italy, the slow advance against a determined enemy in the Scheldt, the final breakthrough over the Rhine and into the heart of Germany, and the triumph of a sweeping victory. The glory of those years was not without its high price, and many of the Canadian Film and Photo Unit recording the war for history were included in the final cost. With this book, I would especially like to remember the photographers who died in action, as well as all the men of the Canadian Armed Forces who still lie in faraway lands.

To do a book of this magnitude requires the assistance of many organizations and talented people. First, I would like to thank the Imperial War Museum in London, the Bundesarchiv of the Federal Republic of Germany in Koblenz, and the American National Archives in Washington. I should particularly like to mention Andrew Birrell, Joy Houston, and Peter Robertson of the National Archives of Canada. Also, I must thank those who helped me at the University of Toronto Press, including Peter Scaggs (Production), Audrey Livernois (Marketing), editors Virgil Duff and Jim Polk, and Don Fernley, the book's designer.

I am grateful for the generous assistance of Col. John Massingham, Mary E. Wright, Fred Moffatt, Col. Robert Douglas, Olga-Dey Bergmoser, Peter Uccello and Sidney Allinson. My thanks to the Historical Section G.S., Ottawa for end paper maps information. I should also like to thank the people of Italy, France, Belgium, and Holland for the warm hospitality shown to me on each of my many trips to Europe. For their special contributions, I am indebted to HRH Prince Bernhard of the Netherlands; Ross Munro; the Countess and Count Yves du Monceau de Bergendal of Brussels; the family Hergaux of Thaon, Normandy; M. Jacques Vico of Abbaye d'Ardenne; Madeleine Nicod and Thérèse Fraeys of Bruges; André Heintz of Caen; and M.E. Mallenquery of Elbeuf.

I am grateful to all the members of the French Resistance Maquis who kindly helped my photographic ventures, and to everyone who patiently allowed me to photograph them. Without their contribution, and the support of many other friends and colleagues too numerous to mention here, this book would not have been possible.

KEN BELL

FOREWORD

This is the definitive pictorial account of Canada's military effort in Europe in the Second World War.

In a remarkable presentation of photographs, many of which have never been published before, the story of our fighting men is vividly recalled, four decades after the conflict ended.

The 450 photos graphically illustrate the tortured raid on Dieppe by our 2nd Division, the spectacular successes of the 1st Division in Sicily, and the ensuing struggle to slug our way up through Italy. Here, too, is the 3rd Division's D-Day assault in Normandy, and our army's fierce campaign on the left of the Allied line across northwest Europe to open the Scheldt to Antwerp. There are remarkable and disturbing photographs which take us back to the crossing of the Rhine, the liberation of Holland, and the final destruction of the Third Reich in the ruins of Germany.

I was a witness to many of the actions in this searing drama, an unforgettable moment in history for anyone who lived through it. Tragically, many young lives did not survive to share their memories, but the legacy they have bequeathed must be a source of enduring pride to all Canadians.

Ken Bell, a consummate photographer who landed with the troops on D-Day in Normandy, has spent five years preparing this powerful record, researching material from Canadian, German, American, and British archives, as well as from combat cinefilm. To add a modern perspective, interspersed in the pictorial narrative are 200 coloured photos of the same places, and sometimes the same people, as they are today.

The Way We Were is a splendid book of pictures by a fine photographer, but more than that, it offers us an evocative reminder of the cost and the carnage of war and the durability of the human spirit. For all of us who must live today in the shadow of nuclear holocaust, these photographs constitute a necessary and eloquent cry for continued peace in an uncertain world.

ROSS MUNRO

Ross Munro has been a war correspondent and a peace-time newspaper publisher.

DIEPPE

For Canadians, the raid on the French port of Dieppe was one of the great disasters of the war. Poorly planned and badly executed, the amphibious attack left 3,363 casualties and prisoners of war out of a total Canadian force of 4,961, whereas German losses for all their services came to 591. Today, it seems hard to believe that any sane military mind could have planned a frontal attack on such a forbidding target. Dieppe's stony beaches are walled by high limestone cliffs, which the Germans had turned into a fortress of barbed wire and concrete bunkers. With sweeping views of the beach, the well-manned enemy positions contained full batteries of artillery, mortar, and machine-guns. The Allies arrived without any pre-battle air bombardment and only minimal naval support. A majority of the men had no combat experience, and their orders left little room for initiative or creative strategies. The result was, predictably, a military disaster.

A number of factors had combined to make this raid seem necessary. By early 1942, the Americans were anxious to develop a second front in Europe, while for some time the Russians had been pushing the Allies to ease pressure on the Eastern Front. The Canadian Army, restless after three years of training in England, felt ready and eager to take a good crack at the Germans. Studying the coastline across the English Channel, Lord Mountbatten considered a flanking attack on Dieppe through villages to the east and west, but somehow it was reported that only second-rate German troops were manning feeble defences. Thus the ill-fated plan for a frontal attack was adopted in mid-May, with Maj.-Gen. J.H. Roberts to command the 2nd Canadian Infantry Division, Capt. J. Hughes Hallett the Naval Force, and Air Vice-Marshal T.L. Leigh-Mallory the Air Forces.

The troops boarded their ships on 3 July, but the weather was so bad that the raid was postponed 24 hours. Weather conditions required yet another postponement, and on 7 July, a German air raid hit two landing-craft carrying Royal Regiment men. Fortunately the bombs passed through the ships before exploding, creating a few casualties, but this, as well as persistent bad weather, led to the cancellation of the entire operation. Troops thoroughly briefed on all the details were then given leave throughout England, jeopardizing any possible hope of complete secrecy about the mission. As Gen. Montgomery said, before leaving for North Africa: 'It should be cancelled for all time.'

However, Allied pressures continued, and the raid was remounted for 19 August 1942, under the code name 'Jubilee.' The landing force comprised some 5,000 Canadians, 1,000 British,

and 50 Americans from the 1st Ranger Battalion. The naval flotilla, including four small destroyers, one gunboat, seven LCIs, and assorted small craft, set sail from England on the evening of 18 August. Unluckily, the crafts carrying the 3rd Commando Battalion, which was to silence the coastal batteries at Berneval on the east flank, met a German convoy in the night, and the ensuing battle not only damaged some of the ships, but greatly upset chances of any surprise attack. In spite of this unfortunate setback, what was left of No. 3 Commando led by Maj. Peter Young miraculously managed to scale the cliffs and reach the big guns. At the same time, No. 4 Commando, led by Lord Lovat, landed on Orange Beach with some American Rangers, at Vasterival. No. 4 was successful in silencing the batteries ahead of the main attack, one of the few bright spots in an otherwise dark day.

After a mixup in their landing-craft formation, the first wave of the Royal Regiment of Canada was 17 minutes late hitting the beach at Puys. It was just after daylight now, and the invaders were easily visible to the enemy, who opened fire before the men hit the code-named 'Blue Beach.' Many were killed before they hit shore. Those who made it got caught in a murderous cross-fire from the pillboxes and bunkers, as well as a deadly hail of mortar and grenades from above. Having no other choice, the Royals had to dash for cover to the base of the sea-wall cliffs. In a valiant effort, a small group led by Lt-Col. Doug Catto got up the hillside, using bangalore torpedoes to clear the barbed wire, only to be pinned down at the top and forced to surrender. Below, those who tried to board the returning landing-craft either were shot or had their boat blown out of the water. Only three of the Royals who landed managed to get back to England that day.

Meanwhile, to the west, the South Saskatchewan Regiment was to land at Pourville. Half an hour later the Queen's Own Cameron Highlanders of Canada were supposed to pass through the South Saskatchewan Regiment and hook up with the Calgary Tanks for an attack on the aerodrome. However, the bridge over the Scie River came under enemy fire, and, despite great bravery from Lt-Col. Cecil Merritt – who received the Victoria Cross for his action in leading men across the bridge – the plan was frustrated. The Camerons moving through the SSR took the west headland, reaching their objective under Maj. Claude Orme in one of the rare successes of the battle.

Since the flanking attacks had failed, the regiments on the beach were rendered particularly vulnerable, especially the Royal Hamilton Light Infantry and the Essex Scottish. When the 27 Churchill tanks of the Calgary Regiment landed, many threw their tracks on the stony beach or were stopped by the anti-tank ditches. The tanks became sitting ducks for enemy fire, the men inside sacrifices to poor military planning. Despite the slaughter, members of the RHLI managed to get to the Dieppe Casino and clear it of the enemy for a time, while a dozen of the Essex Scottish pushed ahead into the town. Hearing of these small victories, the headquarters ship decided to send in reserve troops – Les Fusiliers de Mont-Royal and the Royal Marines. It was a tragic error, a complete waste of men. Dieppe was a death-trap.

The Allied withdrawal action at sea continued, with the landing-craft under heavy fire and many men wounded or drowned, despite the courageous efforts of the Navy and Air Force in covering the operation. As Col. Charles Stacey has said, 'The conditions of evacuation were without parallel in the history of warfare.' By 8:30, 'Operation Jubilee' was all but over, the beaches strewn with limbs and bleeding bodies. The fighting died out shortly after noon, and Germans started rounding up prisoners, looking after the dead and wounded from both sides, and checking out the battered Allied equipment. At 10 minutes past one, the message was finally circulated: 'Our people have surrendered.'

The raid at Dieppe offers much for the military strategist to reflect upon. Such a bold amphibious operation against a fortified port must never be attempted. It is important that any landing deploy massive forces, vigorous naval and air support, seasoned troops, and imaginative planning. Obviously lessons were learned at Dieppe, but yet, can any lesson justify the senseless sacrifice of so many young soldiers? By now, too many Canadians have forgotten Dieppe altogether, but the full horror of the debacle should remain firmly in our memories, or we will have betrayed the men who so tragically perished on its beaches.

The quiet beaches of Dieppe, 1942.

These photographs, taken by German soldiers following the battle, show the damage inflicted on the Canadians during their futile attack against the heavily fortified port of Dieppe.

Landing-craft tanks burn helplessly while bodies lie scattered over the stony shore; and a German officer, a soldier, and some civilians look over the carnage surrounding the burned-out Churchill tank.

Opposite The sun shines again on the beaches at Dieppe.

Little girls play a game of follow-the-leader in the beautiful park where the old Dieppe Casino once stood.

The enemy was prepared and waiting.

A proud German sentry looks out towards a half-submerged Churchill tank.

Badly wounded Canadians lie on the beach waiting to be moved.

A German medic dresses a Canadian's leg wound.

The dead and wounded are moved to the base of the fortified sea-wall as the Germans make preparations to get them to the top.

Prisoners are paraded through
Dieppe under heavy guard,
on their way to prisoner-of-
war camps or to the hospital
in the convent.

The hospital still stands, but visitors buy flowers where war casualties once were tended.

The streets and shops are bustling in this popular holiday centre today.

Former POWs meet regularly to reminisce and to petition the government for more assistance and recognition for their years of brutal imprisonment.

The Germans proudly swap tales of their victory.

A happy German guard marches prisoners to camp.

Field Marshal Gerd von Rundstedt, Commander of the German Army in the West, stands on the beach with his staff and relives the victory.

Above Three German guards pose for photographs in front of their Canadian prisoners.

Below At the hospital, German guards watch as a badly wounded Canadian is lifted from a truck by his buddies.

At Pourville, outside Dieppe, wounded Canadians lie at the side of the road as the battle continues in the background.

The road to the POW camp: prisoners rest in the grass.

Inset Capt. John Foote, Padre of the Royal Hamilton Light Infantry, before boarding his landing-craft for Dieppe. Padre Foote performed heroically on the beach, working under constant fire to bring the wounded back to the landing-crafts and repeatedly returning to the battle. When the Allies finally withdrew, he refused to leave the many helpless and injured who needed his care, and for his bravery was awarded the Victoria Cross.

Decades later, Col. Foote relaxes at home in Cobourg with his cello.

The German burial parade was shunned by the French. The streets are all but deserted and a cyclist deliberately turns his back.

In striking contrast, the return of the Canadians in September 1944 with the same regiments which fought here on 19 August 1942 brought out throngs of the populace to celebrate their new freedom. Here the French cheer and toss flowers as troops march past Gen. H.D.G. Crerar GOC 1st Canadian Army.

The remaining section of the dismantled gun turret is now a tourist resting place.

Pte E.W. Pritchard examines a German gun position with a perfect view of the main beach and a deadly field of fire.

Two years after the raid, the Royal Regiment of Canada returns to Puys. Capt. E.L. McGivern and Capt. J.M. Medhurst check out the pillbox which helped decimate their regiment in the unsuccessful attempt to secure a firm foothold.

Top left Maj. Brian McCool of the Royals was beachmaster at Puys and a POW leader to his men during more than three years of captivity. At the 25th anniversary of the battle, he climbs into the gun position where the Germans wreaked such havoc on his men.

Above Today the beaches belong to another generation, a place for tourists, motor-cyclists, mothers, children, and young lovers.

Left Maj. McCool in Iceland, 1940, with the Regiment's mascot, 'Sgt Royal.'

SICILY

The invasion of Sicily, code-named 'Husky,' was designed to knock Italy out of the war and to tie down German divisions in the south, paving the way for future Allied operations in northwest Europe. The 1st Canadian Infantry Division and the 1st Canadian Army Tank Brigade, trained on the moors and beaches of England, were sent to join the famous 8th Army as part of the 30th British Corps commanded by Lt-Gen. Sir Oliver Leese. The Canadians sailed directly from the River Clyde in June to rendezvous with the Allies in the Mediterranean, but the trip unfortunately cost them three ships off the North African coast, attacked by German U-boats, with 55 Canadians killed and 500 vehicles and artillery units lost.

Despite this set-back, the Canadians arrived to join the assault forces moving slowly towards Sicily on 9 July. The Allied invasion was spotted and reported to the German commander-in-chief but, fortunately, the Sicilian coastal area was defended by Italian troops with little taste for fighting such a force. There was minimal opposition to the landings on the morning of 10 July and Allied objectives were taken with few casualties. As planned, the British Army attacked on the right in the area of Pozallo and then headed up the coast towards Syracuse and Catania. The American 7th Army under Gen. George Patton landed on the western beaches at Gila and Icata, and moved towards Palermo. Both armies were commanded by Gen. Harold Alexander, commander-in-chief of the 15th Army Group. The Canadians, under Gen. Guy Simonds, were responsible for the area around Pachino and its airfield. The first significant breach in the southern wall of 'Fortress Europe' had been made with comparative ease.

On 11 July, the German forces reacted, as the Hermann Goering Panzer Division and the 15th Panzer Grenadier Division fiercely counter-attacked at Gila. The Americans held, and the Germans had to withdraw, planning now to throw the bulk of their forces at the British coming up the east coast. This they did, moving strong elements towards the Canadians and the 51st Highland Division to prevent them from breaking north and hooking up with the Americans. The Germans fought well in the rugged mountain terrain of central Sicily, skilfully selecting defensive positions and delaying the Allied advance with shrewdly placed mines and demolitions. Strengthened by reinforcements from the 1st Parachute Division and the 29th Panzer Grenadier Division, the Germans dug in, and for the Allies each advance in Sicily now became a difficult struggle.

Through Caltagirone, Piazza Armerina, Leonforte, Nossoria, and Assora, Canadians pushed on in the searing July heat, plagued by dust, narrow roads, and blown bridges, taking village after village, many of them perched on craggy mountain tops and stubbornly defended. It was a test of any army continually to keep breaking through the enemy's strong positions, capture, and then hold against severe counter-attacks supported by mortar and artillery fire. Leonforte and Assora, in particular, were taken only after fierce combat and heavy casualties. Near Adrano, the anchor of the German defensive line at the base of Mount Etna, the Canadians turned towards Agira, which was protected by a ring of strongly defended hills. The Edmontons and Patricias cleared Agira, while the 1st Brigade had its hands full at Regalbuto, a few miles east, where the Hermann Goering Division had hidden its tanks among the ancient ruins and were using them as pillboxes.

By the beginning of August, the Allies were closing in on Messina, the town at the Strait of Messina, just across from the toe of Italy's boot. The British had finally entered Catania, and the Americans had taken Troina to the north of Adrano. On 16 and 17 August, the Allies entered Messina, and at last the war in Sicily was over, after 38 days of bitter fighting. In treacherous country, under incredibly difficult conditions, the men of the Canadian 1st Division and the 1st Tank Brigade with their support troops had acquitted themselves with imagination and daring. The price, however, was high: Canadian casualties were 2,434, including 485 all ranks killed.

The German soldier was well-trained, well-equipped, and particularly skilful in defence and retreat, as the Allies were to discover in the long battle through the hills and valleys of Sicily and Italy.

On 10 July, the Allies landed on the soft underbelly of Europe. With very little resistance, the Canadians took Pachino; the Americans on the left headed toward Palermo; and the British on the right moved up the coast to Syracuse.

The sunny beaches and picturesque shops at Pachino now drowse peacefully in the heat of a Sicilian summer.

Opposition stiffened with the arrival of seasoned German troops, and an alert Canadian patrol advances cautiously through fields of waist-high wildflowers.

Overleaf Village by village, the Canadians fought their way north into the mountains of central Sicily, where the retreating enemy countered with mines, booby traps, and a skilful rearguard action.

Children again play games on the Sicilian streets as the older men sit on benches and discuss world events, politics, and perhaps even the war.

31

Chester Helgason and Bob Middleton, now retired in Oakville
and Mississauga, Ontario, have remained good friends.

Princess Patricia's Canadian
Light Infantry runs into heavy
shellfire north of Valguarnera.
Pte C. Helgason is lifted to a
stretcher; the medic at his feet
is Pte R. Middleton. Another
casualty is attended to in the
background.

Agira has changed very little since the war years. On a hill at the outskirts of town stands the Canadian Cemetery, last resting place for the many killed in the fierce mountain fighting.

A PPCLI patrol moves cautiously up the main street of Agira in the mountains of Sicily.

Maj.-Gen. G.G. Simonds, brilliant young commander of the Canadian 1st Division, was later to command the 2nd Canadian Corps in northwest Europe and was acting GOC 1st Canadian Army during the Scheldt operations.

For many years Honorary Col. of the Royal Regiment of Canada, here in full dress scarlet, he is presenting awards to the Regiment at their annual Sorrel Day Parade, held to commemorate the battle of Mount Sorrel in the First World War.

Lt-Col. B.M. Hoffmeister, another brilliant young commander, leads his battalion, the Seaforth Highlanders, up the Sicilian hills at Militello to a rendezvous with Gen. Bernard Montgomery.
Now in retirement in West Vancouver, Maj.-Gen. Hoffmeister, who later took command of the 5th Canadian Armoured Division in Italy and northwest Europe, was selected to command the 6th Division in the Pacific. However, following the surrender of Japan, he retired from the Army and later became president of Macmillan Bloedel Building Materials Limited.

The first church parade for Canadian troops in Sicily was held
in the historic ruins of the Teatro Graeco in Taormina.

Today, Taormina, under the shadow of Mt Etna, is a Mediterranean tourist haven.

ITALY

The Canadians, as part of the 8th Army, were to land on the toe of Italy at Reggio di Calabria, with the British 5th Division to their left opposite Messina. Before dawn on 3 September, the Canadians crossed the Strait of Messina covered by hundreds of guns firing from Sicily to the mainland. Some craft became confused in the darkness as to the correct beach, but it made little difference, since the Italian defence forces had no desire to fight. There was even less trouble here than in the soft landings in Sicily. The Canadians were soon able to move off the beaches and up into the rugged hills beyond.

On 9 September, the US 5th Army, made up of one American and one British corps under Lt-Gen. Mark Clark, would land in the Gulf of Salerno south of Naples, while the British 1st Airborne Division was to land by sea at the heel of the Italian peninsula at Taranto. On 8 September, Italy surrendered and immediately the Germans disarmed all Italian troops and took over their defensive positions. The battle on the beaches of Salerno had turned into a raging inferno, one of the most violent battles of the campaign, and it became clear that the 8th Army would have to move up and take some pressure off the US Army trying to hold its beach-head. The 5th British Division made contact with the American troops on 16 September and, with the fire-power of the British battleships and the stubborn defence of the 5th Army, the German counter-attacks petered out and the initial danger passed.

The Canadian 3rd Brigade, after a record dash through the mountains, took the key road and rail junction city of Potenza on 20 September, while the 1st Brigade, moving to the east, had the Princess Louise Dragoon Guards make contact with the British airborne troops at Taranto. On 1 October, Naples fell to the 5th Army while units of the British 5th Corps on the Adriatic coast speeded north to capture the much-needed airfields on the plains of Foggia. These two armies formed a line across southern Italy, and the Canadians now had to swing westwards into the Matese Mountains, the most formidable seen up to this time. Their task was to take the towns of Vorturara, Campobasso, and Vinchiatura. This they accomplished, but only after the most severe fighting, with many casualties. The terrain was ideally suited for defensive warfare and the German paratroops made the Canadians fight for every inch of ground as they backed slowly towards the Sangro River. Campobasso fell to the 1st Brigade on 14 October, and the next day Vinchiaturo was taken by the 2nd Brigade.

A seaborne landing was made at Termoli on the Adriatic coast to get troops in behind the German lines with the Special Service Brigade and two brigades of 78th British Division. The 16th Pan-

zer Division struck fiercely at this shaky bridgehead, and the fighting was violent as the British were forced to give ground. It was fortunate that the tanks of the Three Rivers Regiment of 1st Canadian Tank Brigade had just arrived by sea from the Italian west coast. They joined the battle at the Biferno bridge and tank action continued all the following day. By nightfall, the 16th Panzers had withdrawn and Termoli and the mouth of the Biferno River were in Allied hands.

At this time, Gen. Simonds was given command of the newly arrived 5th Armoured Division and Maj.-Gen. Vokes took command of the 1st Canadian Infantry Division. In early December the Canadians under Gen. Vokes took over the right flank of the British 5th Corps, north of the Sangro River, and now looked down at the valley of the Moro River and, a few miles beyond, the Adriatic port of Ortona. Most of December was taken up with the contest for this area, where Canadians had to battle against the elements as well as with the elite German paratroops. Under a ceaseless cold rain, the terrain became a quagmire; roads disappeared in the mud and small rivers swelled to rushing torrents. The fighting became more deadly as the troops battled for San Leonardo and Casa Berardi, and the number of killed and wounded swiftly rose. Finally, Capt. Paul Triquet and his company from the Royal 22e Regiment, and a squadron of Ontario Regiment tanks, made a bridgehead over the Moro, a position soon consolidated when reinforcements arrived.

As the Canadians moved towards Ortona, they were preceded by heavy air bombardments on the fanatical German defenders of the port. As the fighting continued, street by street, the paratroopers used the rubble created by our bombings to their advantage as machine-gun nests and cover for snipers. Booby traps, trip-wires, hand-grenades, and fire-bombs all came into action as troops fought in savage hand-to-hand combat. High explosives used to blast walls out of the houses were followed by machine-gun volleys, and tanks of the Three Rivers Regiment were firing at point-blank range to blast paratroopers from their nests. After seven days of fierce fighting, on 27 December, the enemy pulled out of Ortona, leaving rubble and corpses for the exhausted Canadians.

At this stage, the troops had a welcome period of rest and reorganization as the 1st Canadian Corps came into the field under Lt-Gen. H.D.G. Crerar, with 1st Division under Maj.-Gen. Vokes. Maj.-Gen. Burns took over the 5th Armoured Division from Maj.-Gen. Simonds, who was returned to England for future operations. The 1st Canadian Armoured Brigade stayed under the command of the British 13th Corps. As the preparations increased in England for the planned invasion of northwest Europe, the Italian campaign was fast becoming of secondary importance. There was, however, plenty of fighting left for the troops in Italy before they would join their comrades in Holland in early 1945.

In the offensive operations of May 1944, the drive up the Liri Valley towards Rome, men fighting for the first time as a Canadian corps were to play an integral role. The first barrier, the Gustav Line, fortified along the Gari River, was attacked on 11 May with the thunderous roar of a thousand guns opening fire on the enemy. After four days of savage fighting, the 13th British Corps with the 1st Canadian Armoured Brigade broke through the Gustav line from Cassino to the sea. After many months of some of the toughest fighting of the war, Cassino was cut off by a giant pincer movement from the Polish Corps and the 13th British Corps, but not before the survivors of the German 1st Parachute Division had made good their escape to the north.

The Canadian Corps was given the task of breaking the next formidable barrier, the Adolph Hitler Line. The battle was grim, with a murderous rain of machine-gun and mortar fire so devastating that many of the units were reduced to skeleton strength. A breach was finally made in the defences and tank squadrons of the 5th Canadian Armoured Division under Maj.-Gen. Hoffmeister exploited this hard-won opening to roll through to the plains beyond. The Germans again made a stubborn stand at the Melfa River, but the Canadians were not to be denied, and after vicious fighting and many casualties they secured a bridgehead over the river and held. The battle of the Liri Valley was over.

Now the pursuit of the enemy towards the capital began. The Canadian Corps was withdrawn into Army Reserve and the entry into Rome was made by units of the US 5th Army from the Anzio bridgehead, including Canadians of the First Special Service Force. Two days after this, 'Operation Overlord,' the landings on the coast of Normandy, took place. There were still important battles to be fought in northern Italy – the Gothic Line, the Savio River, Ravenna – and it was even more important now to keep Germans tied down on the Italian front as the Allies moved through Normandy. Although almost forgotten, the Canadians kept their winning record intact, holding to the aggressive approach they had maintained from the shores of Sicily through to Messina and up the spine of Italy, fighting mile by mile against a strong and resourceful enemy, until their final victories on the Italian northern plains. It was a glorious record, but not without its cost: a total of more than 25,000 casualties, of whom almost 6,000 still sleep in the fertile soil of Italy.

Clearing villages of snipers and booby traps became routine, as the troops moved up the mountainous back of Italy.

Opposite On 3 September 1943, at the Strait of Messina, with the rugged Calabrian hills in the background, the invading convoy crossing from Sicily to Reggio di Calabria met with even less resistance than it had encountered at Pachino. Today, only a fishing boat patrols these waters.

Canadians moved swiftly up the toe of Italy in an attempt to ease the pressure on the British airborne troops at Taranto and to support the US 5th Army, comprising the 6th US Corps and the British 10th Corps, who were in trouble at Salerno.

Pushing forward through the mountains, the 3rd Canadian
Infantry Brigade took Potenza, an important road junction half-
way between Taranto and Salerno, on 20 September. Here, a
tank of the Calgary Regiment fires in support of the advance of
the West Nova Scotia Regiment.

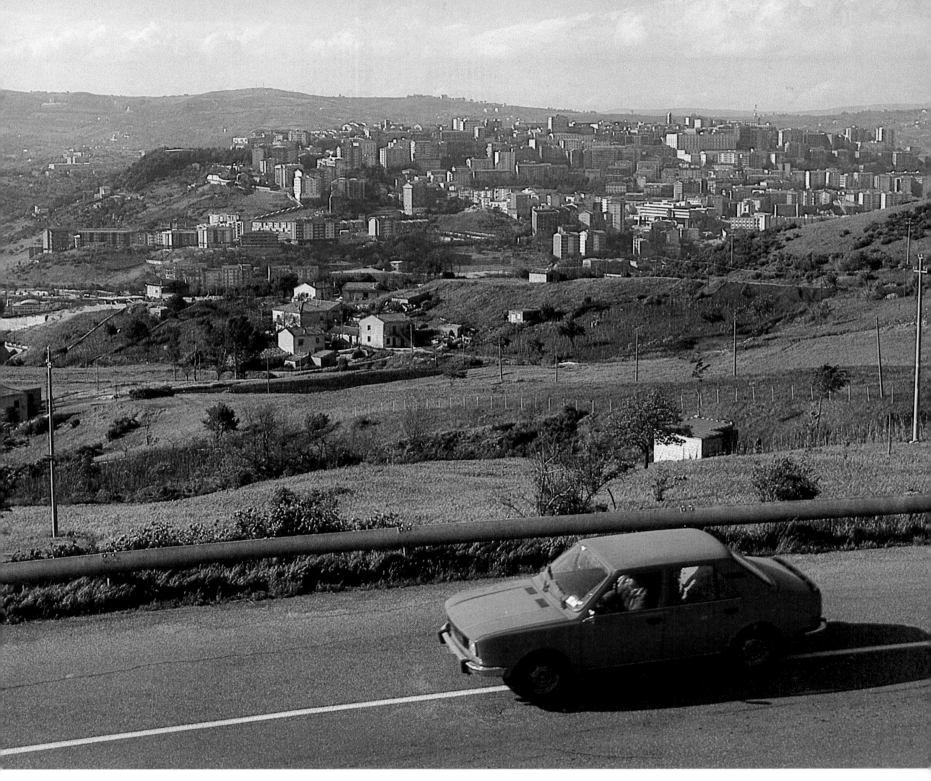

Potenza has grown, but has not lost the quiet charm of a
southern Italian valley town.

Men of the village quietly discuss local events as they walk along a mine-free road.

Campochiaro has few reminders of the life-and-death struggle that took place on these steps so long ago.

A Sherman tank gets minor repairs as it waits for engineers to clear mines from the road ahead.

The Carlton and York Regiment flush out stubborn snipers in the village of Campochiaro. One soldier has already fallen victim.

Top left Landing-craft burns from shellfire during the amphibious assault at Anzio, 22 January 1944.
Top right Field Marshal Sir Harold Alexander confers with officers at Anzio.
Bottom left Flak firing at enemy planes as they threaten the assault crafts.
Bottom right Part of the 6th US Corps of the 5th Army coming ashore against stiff opposition.

Opposite CINE photos of the landing at Salerno on 9 September, one of the fiercest battles of the Mediterranean Campaign. This Anglo-American force formed the US 5th Army, commanded by Gen. Mark Clark, which became the amphibious force deployed at Anzio a few months later.

The people of Naples were starved and begging in the streets by the time the city was freed by the 5th Army.

The lovers on the bench do not remember the war, nor do
most of the members of the new generation in southern Italy.

The battle continued day and night, as the Germans skilfully employed every defensive advantage. Given the rugged terrain, the blown bridges, and the snipers and mines, it was a long, draining struggle. Always one more hill to take, one more river to cross!

Even in the most modern of wars, the sure-footed mule plays his part. In places where vehicles could not travel, mule trains carried food, supplies, ammunition, wireless equipment, mortars, and all other necessities of battle.

Canadian stretcher-bearers remove the wounded under fire and bring a casualty suffering from shock into the Regimental Aid Post.

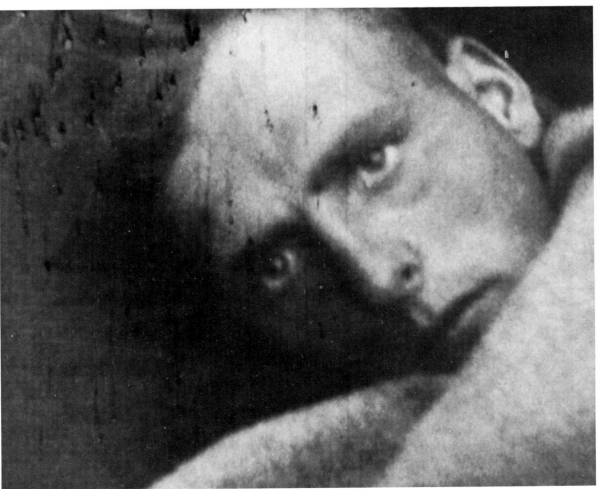

Opposite German machine-gun night-firing in the area of the Hitler Line lights up the Liri Valley.

New Zealand troops fire an anti-tank gun and advance towards the enemy as the Allies make yet another attempt at taking Monte Cassino. This German stronghold, 1,415 feet high, withstood everything the Allied troops threw at it for many frustrating months.

2,500 tons of bombs were dropped on Monte Cassino, 3 March 1944, yet the German paratroops still held tenaciously to their battered defences.

When Monte Cassino was taken on 18 May, it was little more
than bombed-out rubble; the monastery is shown with the Polish
flag flying on top. The Allied and Commonwealth Cemetery includes
the dead of most of the nations that fought so valiantly here.

The quiet streets of Ortona are perfect for a quick kiss as young lovers unknowingly walk by a house scarred by the war.

Opposite These war-film photos show the vicious seven-day battle over Christmas 1943 which took place in Ortona. The troops advanced, house by house, with bayonet, rifle, and grenade, no quarter asked and none given.

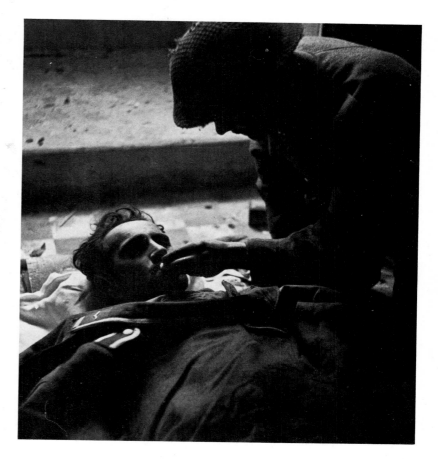

Two soldiers fire at a sniper around the corner, as a wounded
German is helped by a medical orderly.

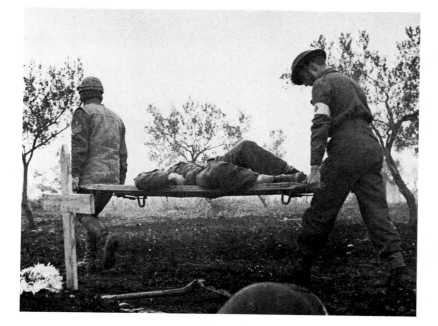

Opposite German machine-
gunners with a camera
mounted on their gun catch
the killing of Canadians at the
Moro River.

The magnificent church of Ortona was cut in half by bombs and shelling during the week-long battle for the city.

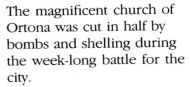

A wounded soldier is helped back to a casualty clearing station at the Hitler Line in the Liri Valley.

The church has been rebuilt and looks down on the busy market-place where the *polizia* keep all in order.

Canadian troops advancing on the hills before Rome.

Tanks and equipment had trouble with the treacherous muddy terrain.

Cpl 'Smokey' Smith, Seaforth Highlander, won the Victoria Cross at the Savio River crossing for his heroic actions against enemy tanks.

Sgt Smokey Smith in front of his very successful travel agency in downtown Vancouver.

Capt. Paul Triquet, Royal 22e Regiment, won the first Victoria Cross awarded in the Mediterranean theatre for his courage at Casa Berardi on the road to Ortona.

Maj. Paul Triquet, now deceased, was photographed at the Royal Canadian Military Institute at a dinner for the thirteen surviving recipients of the Victoria Cross.

D-DAY

When dawn broke over the English Channel on 6 June 1944, the cold light unveiled the largest armada of ships the world has ever seen: more than 5,000 craft moving slowly towards the coast of Normandy. This mighty force, protected by an umbrella of over 2,000 aircraft and the escort ships of the Royal Navy, inched relentlessly toward the French beaches, the 15-inch guns of the *Warspite* and the *Ramillies* relentlessly hammering away at the enemy defences inland. After intensive planning and preparation, 'Operation Overlord' was under way.

Beyond the sea-walls, three airborne divisions had landed in the rear of the assault, among them the 6th British Airborne Division which included the 1st Canadian Parachute Battalion. Their mission was to seize bridges and otherwise disconcert the enemy behind the line of attack. The landing forces on the beach included the Canadian 3rd Division and the 2nd Armoured Brigade as part of Gen. Miles Dempsey's 2nd British Army. The Canadians were in the centre at Juno Beach and flanked by the British 3rd Division at Sword Beach and the 50th Northumbrian Division on the right at Gold Beach. To the west, the 1st US Army was landing under Gen. Omar Bradley at Omaha and Utah beaches.

This was the invasion that dare not fail, and all the troops knew it. Gen. Eisenhower, worried deeply about bad weather conditions, on 5 June had to decide it was now or never, although bad weather continued. Fortunately, all the landings went as planned, with the exception of the US 5th Corps' landing at Omaha Beach, which ran into a German division on an anti-invasion exercise. The Germans, surprised to discover themselves in the real thing, opened fire on the troops and the Americans found it tough going to get a foothold on the beach. In the Canadian sector, the Germans stubbornly held out in the area of Courseulles, and the Regina Rifles got involved in heavy street fighting. At Bernières, too, the Queen's Own Rifles met up with determined defenders in concrete gun positions and suffered many casualties; eventually, by storming the sea-wall and outflanking the enemy, they forced a surrender. At Saint-Aubin, the North Shore Regiment also ran into serious opposition, and deadly sniper action went on for most of the day.

By early afternoon, the 3rd Division was ashore on a narrow strip of beach-head, creating much congestion and confusion. After a period of untangling themselves, the troops moved inland to the area of Bény-sur-Mer, the 9th Highland Brigade passing through the 7th and 8th Assault Brigades toward Carpiquet airfield and the city of Caen. A few tanks of the 1st Hussars, with men of the North Nova Scotia Regiment aboard, made it to their objective, the Bayeux-Caen road, but without infantry support they had to retire. It would be another month before Canadians would finally take these objectives.

Despite some set-backs, D-Day was turning into a success. The Allies were helped immeasurably by a conflict of opinion in the German high command. Wise, experienced Field Marshal Gerd von Rundstedt wanted to hold back his reserve armoured divisions for mobile counter-attack, whereas Field Marshal Erwin Rommel believed that any invasion of the beaches should be beaten back immediately, using reserve Panzer divisions with all available fire-power. Rommel had, in fact, built up an almost impregnable defence on the west wall, bristling with guns, but as fate would have it, he was at home with his wife on the day of the landing, preparing for a trip to see Hitler. Von Rundstedt felt the landing was a diversionary tactic and kept waiting for the main force to come from the Pas de Calais area, where the Allies had set up a dummy army, with mock-up tanks 'commanded' by a highly conspicuous Gen. George Patton. Over the wireless, false information was leaked about a supposed buildup of these troops, and von Rundstedt held his Panzer divisions at the ready for a landing which never came.

With clever planning, immense courage, and some welcome good luck, the Allies were finally able to link all their bridgeheads into one continuous front. Casualties were heavy, but not overwhelming, troop morale remained high, and the success of 'Operation Mulberry,' an artifical harbour assembled from giant steel caissons floated across the Channel from Britain, meant the Allies did not have to land near a major port to supply their armies. This man-made harbour was to prove an essential factor in our successes in Normandy. The military had clearly learned something from the mistakes of the Dieppe disaster and D-Day marked the beginning of the end for the German Wehrmacht.

Some of the Luftwaffe break through the Allied air screen to bomb troops landing on Juno Beach.

A few days before D-Day, two Germans look longingly across
the sea to England – so near, and yet so far.

German bombers come out in force in an attempt to stop the
Allied fleet approaching the coast of Normandy.
Bottom The invasion fleet as seen through a German telescope;
the anti-invasion defences are prominent in the foreground.

Landing-craft headed for shore through bombardment from shore batteries. The heavy seas wreaked havoc on some of the D-Day tanks swimming ashore, and many foundered before reaching the beaches.

Opposite Battleships of the Royal Navy fire on the shore defences of the invasion beaches. Five battleships, 2 monitors, 19 cruisers, and 77 destroyers took part in this greatest of all bombardments.

Assault troops leave their landing-craft with bangalore torpedoes, ladders, and a good-luck pat on the back.

Above Today a different type of boat sails towards the Norman beaches and the Orne River. As the afternoon wanes, sun-burned sailors happily return to safe haven.

Right The same beaches are now crowded with weekend holiday-makers and windsurfers.

Opposite Germans fight fiercely to repel the Canadians as they move inland from the beaches. Prisoners are captured and moved to the beach to disembark on landing-crafts for POW camps. In the sea are amphibious tanks that didn't make it to the beach.

Top right The first Bren carrier moves cautiously into Courseulles-sur-Mer, as photographed by French Maquis.

The amphibious Sherman tank of the First Hussars commanded by Sgt Leo Gariepy enters a side-street of Courseulles, searching out the enemy rearguard.

Inset A family strolls along the same street.

The Royal Marine Commandos hit Sword Beach to the left of the Canadians at St Aubin-sur-Mer.

Middlesex Regiment also landing on Sword Beach.

The Royal Marine Commandos move inland to clear their objectives.

The bloodiest fighting of the day was on the 1st US Army 5th Corps front at Omaha Beach, which ran into serious difficulties with a German field division on the coast. The US 7th Corps had a much easier landing to the west on Utah Beach.

Troops of the US 4th Infantry Division wade ashore from landing-crafts off Utah Beach.

Exhausted GIs take a quick break at the base of the sea-wall as fresh troops arrive to keep the pressure on the enemy.

An emergency First Aid Centre develops by the sea-wall as the wounded get hasty medical aid on Omaha Beach.

Above The Highland Light Infantry of the 9th CIB disembark at Bernières-sur-Mer, having been landed at the beach-head by the RCN.
Below The tide is out at Bernières-sur-Mer as windsurfers finish for the day and carry their equipment back to their beach-houses.

German prisoners are escorted by their officers to finish the war in English POW camps.

Badly needed reinforcements arrive to bolster the exhausted assault troops and to keep the pressure on the enemy.

The fish are biting today, and locals and tourists alike are out on the stone pier at the mouth of the River Orne. Meanwhile sailors return to safe anchorage at the marina in Courseulles-sur-Mer.

At the beach of Bernières-sur-Mer, sun-worshippers relax where so many brave Canadians fought and died.

First prisoners are rounded up during the early morning of D-Day at the Bernières railway station, now the local post office and bus depot.

Prisoners and the wounded gather by the gun position in the Queen's Own Rifles landing area. This gun inflicted many casualties before being silenced.

This spot has become a memorial to the Queen's Own, as well as a tourist attraction on the sea-wall.

Maj.-Gen. R.F.L. Keller, commander of the 3rd Canadian Infantry Division in Normandy, lands on the beach and issues orders to his personnel.

More German prisoners are brought in and wait under guard until a landing-craft is ready for the run back to England.

This mansion became a landmark for the invading troops, and was hit many times. Today with beach-houses flanking either side, it stands in the setting sun as a proud survivor of a great period in military history.

The town square in Courseulles soon became a traffic junction for army vehicles and fresh troops. Today the area is bright with flowers and new shops, although there are still those who will never forget the dramatic events of over 40 years ago.

US forces started a rapid buildup of supplies and men in preparation for their dash across the Cherbourg peninsula. The Germans fought desperately to hold their ground, and an area which is now a paradise for the sun-seeker and boating enthusiast once saw bitter military action.

NORMANDY

The ambitious objectives of D-Day called for the British to take Caen and the high ground to the south on the Falaise road, with the 3rd Canadian Infantry Division and the 2nd Canadian Armoured Brigade in support, cutting the Caen-Bayeux road and taking the Caen airfield at Carpiquet. These aims proved out of reach on D-Day. However, on the following morning, 7 June, the Canadians tried again, and the 7th Brigade with very little enemy resistance managed to reach the Caen-Bayeux road. The 9th Brigade, against much stiffer resistance, took Buron and moved on to Authie before it was hit by tanks and infantry of the Panzer Grenadiers. The villages were overrun by the enemy, and after many casualties, the 9th was forced to withdraw to the area of Les Buissons.

On D plus two, another fierce German counter-attack almost destroyed three companies of the Royal Winnipeg Rifles at Putot-en-Bessin. At Bretteville-l'Orgueilleuse the same day, the Regina Rifles were engaged in a night-long battle with German Panther tanks; at a terrible cost, they managed to hold the village and by dawn the tanks had withdrawn. The British met the same kind of opposition on their advance towards Caen, and it would be another month before Caen would fall to the British and Canadians.

By 8 June the Germans had brought in three armoured divisions. Gen. Montgomery as commander of all ground forces in France took advantage of the enemy decision to hold Caen by pressuring the enemy to commit more of its armour in the Caen sector, thus giving the Americans the opportunity to break out into the rest of France. This turned out to be good Allied strategy, but was tough on Canadian and British troops. Through the month of June, they had to fight in the bocage country of Normandy, with its stone walls ideally suited for enemy defences and hedgerows thick enough to stop a tank. In front of the Canadians since D plus one was the 12th SS Panzer Division, the fanatical Hitler Youth, 19-year-olds commanded by Maj.-Gen. Kurt Meyer, who was to stand trial for the murder of 23 men of the 9th CIB, found shot and half-buried, some with their hands tied, in the grounds of L'Abbaye d'Ardenne. Most of the men were from the North Nova Scotia Highlanders and the Sherbrooke Fusiliers. This hated SS unit also committed similar atrocities against captured Canadians from the Regina Rifles, the Queen's Own Rifles, the Winnipeg Rifles, and the 1st Hussars.

During much of June, the Canadian role was primarily to defend the bridgehead while the buildup continued. By the end of June, the Allies had almost a million soldiers in Normandy and 100,000 vehicles. Unfortunately, on 19 June a storm struck the landing beach and the unloading of supplies at the artificial harbour had to be suspended for almost four days. By that time the American harbour was so badly damaged that it never was completed. The British harbour at Arromanches was repaired, however, and in a few days men and supplies began to flow again.

The American Army had now taken the port of Cherbourg, and by the end of June, the 2nd British Army had at least eight German Panzer divisions tied down in the Caen area. The situation remained fluid as Germans and Allies jockeyed for position. Striving to push British and Canadian troops quickly back to the sea, the Germans used smaller units piecemeal, and when the smoke of battle cleared, often very little had changed. The Allies enjoyed a considerable advantage, having almost complete control of the air from airstrips carved out of Normandy's rich wheat fields. Not only could they observe the enemy's movements, but fighter aircraft of the Tactical Air Force were continually blasting German columns of arms and supplies, forcing them to operate by night or suffer huge losses.

By now, the Canadians had become battle-hardened veterans, standing up against the best that the enemy could throw at them. Having to learn the hard way, they knew the importance of a shovel, the sounds of enemy fire, and the techniques of spotting a minefield. With the buildup, they were receiving massive support in fire-power from countless artillery regiments, as well as from the big guns of the Royal Navy off the coast. Now, backed up by countless tanks and improved air surveillance, the seasoned Canadians, along with the 2nd British Army, were ready for their move to Caen. On the German side there was a new player, a Hitler favourite, Field Marshal von Kluge, replacing Field Marshal von Rundstedt, who had dared advise his Fuehrer that the Germans should withdraw.

The first task of the 3rd CID was to capture Carpiquet village and airfield, which had been a D-Day objective a month earlier and was now defended by a group of Hitler Youth. In the early dawn of 4 July, behind a creeping artillery barrage, the Canadian 8th Brigade along with the Royal Winnipeg Rifles moved into the attack supported by the tanks of the 1st Hussars. The day-long action exacted a high toll in dead and wounded, and was only partially successful: Carpiquet village was taken, but full control of the airfield was not to be ours until the fall of Caen itself.

The plan to take Caen was code-named 'Operation Goodwood.' Bomber Command was under Air Chief Marshal Arthur Harris, who decided that instead of bombing in advance of the assault, given the possibility of bad weather, he would bomb the night before, on 7 July. The bomb line was to be 6,000 yards in front of our troops, which left most of the enemy, who were well dug into fortified positions close to our lines, perfectly free of the target area. It was also decided to drop leaflets to the citizens of Caen so they could evacuate the city. Few found it possible to leave and many others paid no heed or had nowhere to go with fighting all around them. The alerted Germans, however, moved across the Orne to the suburbs of Colombelles and Faubourg de Vaucelles, or came forward to prepare for the attack they knew was imminent.

At 10:30 on the night of 7 July, bombers arrived out of the sunset in spectacular waves, dropping two-and-a-half thousand tons of bombs on the northern edge of Caen with thunderous roars that shook the earth. Flames began leaping thousands of feet into the air, a heart-warming sight for the troops in their slit trenches; unfortunately, few men realized that only marginal damage was being done to the enemy they would face in a few hours. Fearful of hitting our front-line troops, the Pathfinders were slowly moving the target line to the south so that the bombing gradually affected most of the city, except for the southern suburbs where the enemy was concentrated. This tragic slaughter of French civilians was completely without justification; the bombardment managed only to take innocent lives and clog the Caen streets with rubble that severely hindered our own progress later on.

Early the next morning, artillery took over in a massive barrage directed at enemy positions, with naval guns offshore contributing fire-power. The 9th CIB moved south once again into Buron, Authie, Gruchy, and Cussy: names familiar from the first days in Normandy. The Highland Light Infantry battled all day against Hitler Youth at 'Bloody Buron,' winning the town but losing 262 men and their colonel. The North Novas were back in Authie, and long past nightfall burning tanks lit up the sky as the vicious struggle went on all along the front.

On the morning of 9 July, men from 9th Canadian Infantry Brigade picked their way carefully into what was left of Caen. The streets were mined and booby-trapped, and German snipers waited patiently behind the heaps of rubble. Caen had been won, but the battle cost Canadian forces 330 dead and 864 wounded, more casualties than the landing on D-Day. Also, the pointless destruction of the city and its people must be seen as one of the saddest mistakes of the war.

A Bren carrier of the South Saskatchewan Regiment brings in a stream of prisoners through the hedgerows of Normandy.

Cameron Highlanders of Ottawa fired continuously through the rows of hedges as the fresh German troops made a concerted effort to break through to the sea. During this two-day engagement, Pte McAllister was killed, and 40 years later his mate on the next gun, young Pte Dixon Raymond, who joined the regiment at 16 from New Jersey, visits his friend's grave at Bény-sur-Mer.

Slit trenches were a way of life and the shovel became as important as the rifle. During bitter day-and-night fighting with SS troops, the area around Gruchy, Authie, and Buron became known as Hell's Corner.

Opposite German resistance stiffened with fresh first-line divisions including the 21st Panzer Grenadier Division and the fanatical Hitler Youth Nazi 12th SS Panzer Division. Fighting behind the stone walls and hedgerows of Calvados, the Canadians were given the task of holding the bridgehead while the buildup continued for a major attack on Caen.

Forty years later, three veteran SDG Highlanders – Grant Richie, Max Sexsmith, and John Pasquino – place a Rue des Glengarrians sign on a corner near Authie.

93

Using a tank as a shield, these soldiers make life-or-death dashes around the corner as the bullets spurt off the stone wall.

Today, two children sit on the pump-handle in front of that same wall.

Lt Garth Webb, 14 Field Regiment, and his exhausted crew, as dawn breaks on the morning of D-Day plus one after a night of continuous firing.

Lt Webb reminisces about the war by a collector's SP tank identical to the one he commanded through northwest Europe 40 years ago.

Sgt Alex Garbutt points to shrapnel holes through the radiator of his 19th Field Regiment ammunition truck, shortly after D-Day.

The war largely forgotten, Alex Garbutt does good deeds for the Lions Club of Etobicoke.

25-pounders of the Belgian brigade attached to the Canadians fire round after round into the German positions.

The 5.5 mediums add their fire to the almost continuous roar of battle, as every effort is made to prevent the enemy from concentrating for another large-scale attack.

Sgt Bill Grant of the Canadian Army Film and Photo Unit had his leg crushed shortly after D-Day. With him is Capt. Colin McDougall and driver Pte M. Treganza.

Inset On the 40th anniversary of D-Day, Bill Grant returns to the same beach at Bernières-sur-Mer.

Two French children, one wearing the Glengarry of the young
SD&G medic who took care of his injured leg.

Padre Capt. R. Seaborne gives absolution to a dying man on the roadside leading to Caen.

A French woman strikes a Canadian POW because of the Allied bombing – or perhaps to impress the German captors.

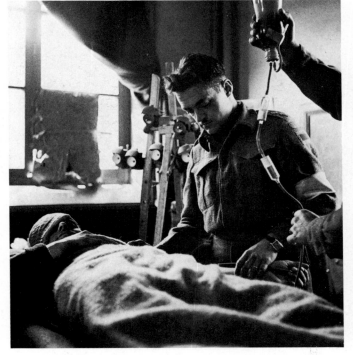

Capt. Earl Bourbonnais of Montreal with the 23rd Field Ambulance gives plasma to a casualty in a makeshift medical room.

Sister I. Ogilvie lights a cigarette for paratrooper Kivinien before flying from the airstrip in Normandy to hospital in England.

Casualties are evacuated aboard a Douglas Dakota flying from a rapidly built airstrip near the beaches of Calvados.

Rocket-bearing 'Typhoons,' the terror of the enemy tanks, fly from the Normandy airstrips.

Jeep ambulances were always on the move from the front to medical evacuation centres.

As the casualties mount, jeep ambulances crowd the dusty roads to evacuate the wounded. In spite of their red crosses, they are not immune to mortar, airbursts, or shellfire.

The Staghound scout car waits while the traffic ahead makes its way through the narrow, rubble-clogged streets of Creully. *Inset* Today the traffic flows freely past the rebuilt church and its monument to the French soldiers of the area who died in the war of 1914–18.

102

General Sir Bernard Montgomery, commander of all the land forces in northwestern Europe, called a press conference on D-Day plus six to give a situation report to the press covering the 2nd British Army Area under Lt-Gen. Sir Miles Dempsey. *Inset* Montgomery retired, relaxing in his rose garden in Isington Mills, England, shortly before his death in 1976.

Few surrendered. Most of the Hitler Youth captured were wounded, and they remained arrogant as prisoners.

The 12th SS Panzer Division, the Hitler Jugend, comprised fanatical young Nazis commanded by Maj.-Gen. Kurt Meyer. These 19-year-old fanatics tried to keep the Canadians from reaching Caen, and it wasn't long before they had established a reputation for ferocious fighting and gratuitous brutality. Canadian POWs from 9 CIB were found in the grounds of L'Abbaye d'Ardenne at Authie, hands tied behind their backs, victims of Hitler Youth.

Armoured scout cars of the Belgian Brigade take a break in
Sallenelles on the Canadians' east flank.

Prince Bernhard of the Netherlands, visiting the area, stops to
talk to a keen young Belgian, 2nd Lt Count Yves du Monceau,
fresh from Sandhurst, England.

The town of Sallenelles has scarcely changed; people still chat on street corners, but not about war.

HRH Prince Bernhard and the now-LCol Count Yves du Monceau, member of the Belgian Senate, meet at the Royal Palace in the Netherlands to talk about the intervening 43 years.

The Highland Light Infantry at rest. Thirsty Highlanders discover a cache of calvados and give it a thorough sampling.

The Padre Rev. 'Jock' Anderson leads a group in a singsong with Capt. Gord Sims on the accordion.

It takes a lot of milk to feed a regiment, and what better way for farm boys like Pte F.E. Calvert and L.Cpl H.G. Murray to show their talents to their buddies?

Top left 40 years later, the veterans led by LCol Ray Hodgins, Croix de Guerre, return to Buron to remember their missing comrades, and the fight against the Hitler Youth.

French children place flowers in front of the memorials to the Sherbrooke Fusiliers and the Highland Light Infantry of Canada.

LCol Rev. Jock Anderson MC and BAR holds a service in memory of the many killed at 'bloody' Buron.

'Hank' Murray, retired, lives in Brantford with his granddaughter, Michelle.

F.E. Calvert, now retired in Chatham, Ontario, is photographed near the Armouries in Cambridge, home of the HLIC.

One of the most important factors in the Allied success in Normandy was the construction in Britain of 'Mulberry Harbour,' which was floated section by section to Arromanches and then assembled. This 'harbour' spelled the difference between being pushed into the sea and winning the battle of the beaches. Violent storms almost completely destroyed it later in June.

Defiant Hitler Youth.

British schoolchildren line up for a class photograph on the heights above Arromanches, the site of the artificial harbour.

Action continues during the final assaults on Caen, with the wounded carried out and a Seaforth piping the troops into battle.

A French woman hit by shrapnel.

A dispatch rider takes shelter behind a tree.

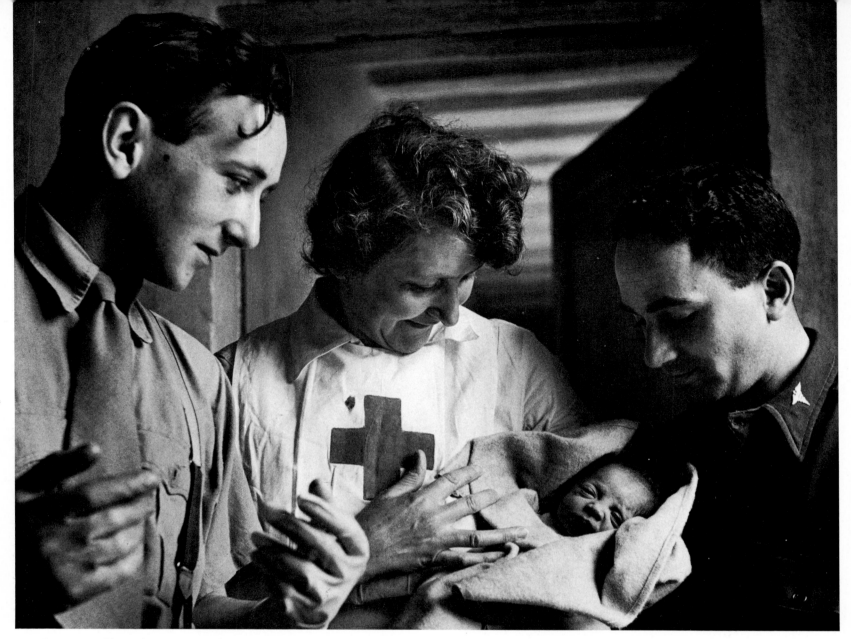

Just born at Villons-les-Boissons: Marie-France, delivered by a US and French medical team and photographed only several minutes old.

On her fifth birthday, her mother combs her hair and she plays in the barnyard with her pet rabbit.

25 years later, Marie-France is holding her son, Fabrice Hergaux.

Fabrice on his motor-bike, with his mother on her 40th birthday.

The family Hergaux's new home in Thaon, not far from Buron. Marie-France, Raymond, and Fabrice are framed in the windows of their new home.

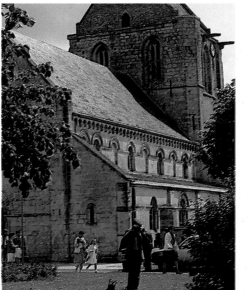

A Bren carrier with camouflaged 6-pound anti-tank guns speeds through the wrecked town of Carpiquet.
Inset Mother and the twins can stroll safely now.

Opposite A soldier pauses before the Virgin and Holy Child in the ancient, damaged Carpiquet church on the outskirts of Caen.

The church of Carpiquet has been completely restored, stone by stone, and after the service, groups enjoy being photographed in their Sunday best.

Caen

As the Canadians entered Caen on the morning of 9 July, some Germans who had infiltrated back into the city, concealed by piles of rubble, began picking off men by sniper fire. After our massed bombing the previous night, tanks could not be brought in until the roads were cleared and bridges built across the River Orne. To the surprise of the troops, after having inflicted so many civilian casualties in the bombing, the men from Canada were greeted by the people of Caen with embraces and flowers, and the soldiers were quick to share their cigarettes and rations of food. There was still fighting to be done at such pockets of resistance as the almost-destroyed railway station, the jail, the city hall, and other points where Germans could delay our street clearing with sniper fire, machine-guns, trip-wires, and booby traps.

In these dangerous street operations, the French Resistance fighters, the Maquis, were invaluable. It was an emotional scene in the tiny square in front of the Church of St Etienne when, in a brief ceremony, men of the Resistance wearing their Cross of Lorraine armbands raised the French flag. Throughout Normandy, the Maquis had been armed with Sten guns and ammunition dropped by air, weapons to be kept hidden until the opportune moment arrived. At Caen they performed extremely well, although elsewhere, in exhilaration at their new-found freedom, the Maquis sometimes overreached themselves and tried to do too much for their small number and lightweight equipment. Sadly, many were killed by the more experienced Germans.

At the same time, in Carpiquet, the Queen's Own Rifles had finally taken the airport which the Canadians had struggled for so desperately since the early days after the landing. However, the enemy retreated across the River Orne to survive and fight another day. In the cloisters of the Abbaye aux Hommes at the cathedral, which had miraculously escaped serious damage from the bombing, more than a thousand refugees huddled on beds of straw with salvaged blankets and whatever scant belongings they had saved. Old folks crouched, still in a daze from the fury of the bombs, trying to comfort children who were weeping and unable to understand why they weren't in their homes – homes which likely no longer existed. There were many wounded and dying, and an emergency hospital was set up in the monks' refectory. More bodies continued to be brought in, as the non-stop task of digging through the chaotic streets uncovered more victims.

Now, ironically, the heavy machinery of the Engineers had to be used to clear the streets, pave the roadways, and build the bridges that we had just destroyed, so that our armour could move forward to support the infantry holding the line on the River Orne. At Dieppe, the Allies had not bombed the city prior to the landings on the beach, fearing that bombardment would alert the enemy, kill civilians, antagonize our allies, and impede the progress of tanks through rubble-filled streets. At Caen we did an about-face, dropping leaflets to warn the populace – and thereby the Germans, of course, who moved out. Our bombs killed scores of French civilians and blocked every street so thoroughly that it took many days and all our Engineers and their heavy equipment to clear a route through the city. Our strategy certainly wasn't very consistent, and we still had the responsibility of burying the dead, looking after the wounded, and feeding the populace.

Meanwhile, 'Operation Goodwood,' now called by the Canadians 'Operation Atlantic,' was not yet completed. The suburbs near the River Orne were still held by German troops and it was of prime importance to clear out these forces before a major advance could be started southward down the axis of the Falaise road. By now the 2nd Canadian Corps was operational, with the arrival of 2nd Canadian Infantry Division and 4th Canadian Armoured Division as Lt-Gen. Simonds set up his tactical headquarters in Amblie, north of Caen. However, the main effort to clear the suburbs south of Caen fell on the shoulders of the 3rd Division. There was bitter fighting in the twisted steel of the bombed industrial factories and the Germans battled as viciously as ever in their defensive role. The 8th and 9th Brigades crossed the Orne below Caen and attacked the enemy in Colombelles while 7th Brigade fought its way from Caen across the river into Faubourg de Vaucelles to join them. There was confusion and heavy action when the Queen's Own Rifles ran into a cluster of machine-gun nests at Giberville, where they suffered tremendous casualties before taking the village and holding it against the inevitable counter-attacks.

Finally all the objectives of 3rd Division were taken and cleared. Maj.-Gen. Foulkes and the newly arrived 2nd Canadian Division passed through the 3rd, and the Royal Regiment of Canada cleared Louvigny after some violent fighting late on 18 July. The following day, Le Régiment de Maisonneuve, although given the wrong start-line, took Fleury sur Orne in their first battle; further to the east, the Black Watch captured the village of Ifs, and the area between the junction of the Orne and the Odon was cleared. Operation Goodwood was completed. The next phase of the Battle of Normandy was to begin the month-long advance down the Falaise road and the closing of the Falaise Gap, at such a terrible cost.

While the Canadians were clearing the suburbs of Caen, two things happened which would have a major bearing on the remainder of the war. Typhoons patrolling the area near Vimoutiers spotted a German staff-car, which they immediately attacked and destroyed. German soldiers nearby pulled the unconscious body of Field Marshal Erwin Rommel from the wreck. Then, three days later, during a top-level conference in Hitler's bunker headquarters in East Prussia, a planted brief-case loaded with explosives blasted the room into shreds. Many were killed, but Hitler, full of shrapnel fragments and deaf from the blast, survived to take revenge on the conspirators. A number of them, and their families, committed suicide, but more than 5,000 died terrible, lingering deaths at the hands of the Gestapo, meant to serve as a lesson to all Germans and particularly to the senior generals.

Now generals could no longer, without being assumed an enemy of the state, ask permission of Hitler to make tactical withdrawals when the need arose. Their fear of the madman at the helm and what he could do to their families and friends began to override any logical decisions on tactical matters. It became a matter of course to ask troops to fight to the death in situations that didn't warrant it, rather than risk crossing Der Fuehrer, who was slowly but surely destroying the mighty forces of Germany with his irrational decisions.

A patrol moves cautiously through the streets of Caen.

Caen, now rebuilt with broad boulevards and expansive parks, has become a thriving university town and business centre. The streets are full of life today, as flags fly to celebrate the 40th anniversary of the Liberation.

Top Caen was taken on 9 July by 1st British Corps, including the Canadian 3rd Division. The preliminary air bombardment almost completely destroyed the city, killing many civilians.

French rescue workers had the grim job of removing the dead from the rubble for many days afterwards.

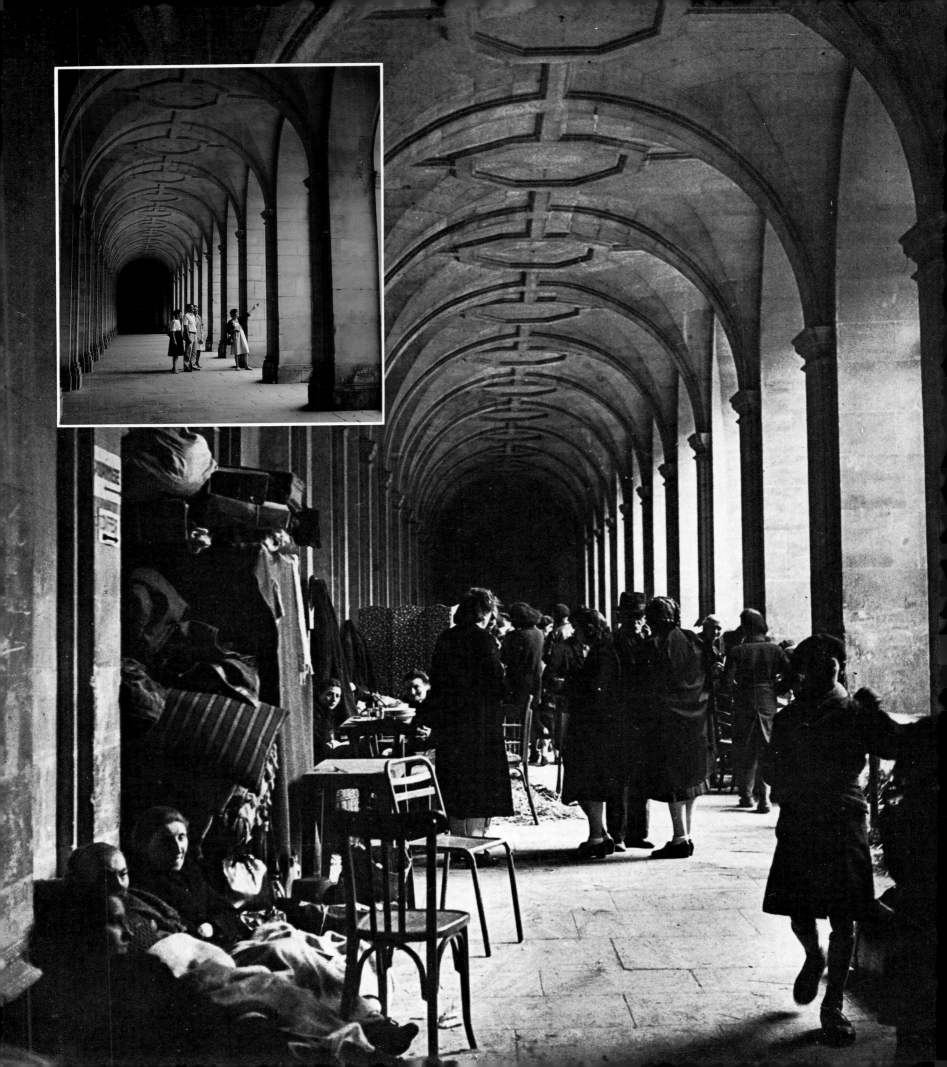

Two women sit in the churchyard with their rosaries during the Bastille Day service.

Most killed in the bombing of Caen were buried in the old cemetery in the churchyard at St Ouen-de-Rots.

A young boy stands with the Canadian Guard of Honour from Régiment de Maisonneuve on this 14th of July, Bastille Day.

Some of the older refugees wait in the interior of the church with a younger woman and her child wrapped in blankets.

Civilians took refuge in the church of St Etienne, the cloisters crowded with the old and the very young with their few pitiful belongings. *Inset* Visitors to the church are taken on a tour, including the cloisters that sheltered so many.

After clearing the Caen railway station, men of the Stormont, Dundas, and Glengarry Highlanders take a short break for a mess-tin dinner.

Men from the Royal 22e Regiment, in Normandy for the 40th Anniversary ceremonies, wait for the train to return to their base in Germany.

The burning jail is checked out very cautiously.

Flower stalls near the old battlements of Caen.

The victor and the vanquished sit in the shattered ruins of the Caen railroad station.
Inset The trains once again are on time.

The canal flows serenely against a background of war's
devastation.

The coiffure shop is still in operation.

The same canal attracts young fishermen now.

Bdr E.I. Hill 2nd Anti-Tank Regiment, was killed here entering Caen. French civilians covered the crumpled body and raised a cairn of cobblestones which became a symbol of the Liberation.

A plaque has replaced the shrine, and each Bastille Day, a ceremony is held here to commemorate Bdr Hill and the Canadians who liberated Caen.

The good Sisters returned with their belongings in a cart.

Survivors struggle to salvage a few pieces of wood – or anything that can help them rebuild.

The Maquis, the fighters of the French Resistance, did valiant work at Caen in aiding the Allies. Armed with Sten guns dropped to them by air, they helped clear the Nazis out of their city. Here they raised the French flag in the square of the church of St Etienne.
Inset left Three survivors of the photographed Maquis are Almire, Tribouellard, and René LeSech.
Inset right Gen. Pierre Michel. In the war photo, he is the figure on the right in the raincoat and beret.

Maple Leaf, the Canadian Army newspaper, found a new home in Caen in the offices of a French newspaper.
Here Lt-Col. Dick Malone is hanging up the new sign with the help of Capt. Placide Labelle.

Col. Richard Malone OBE at the unveiling of the monument of Field Marshal Montgomery in Brussels in 1984.

Capt. Doug MacFarlane, managing editor of *Maple Leaf* in Naples, Rome, Brussels, and Amsterdam, is shown here at work in North Africa.

Maj. MacFarlane MBE is still in the world of newspapers, as well as real estate and business consultancy.

128

Ross Munro, OC OBE, vetran war correspondent, had five amphibious landings: Spitsbergen, Dieppe, Sicily, Italy, and Normandy. He founded, and was the publisher of, *Canadian Magazine*. He was publisher of the Edmonton *Journal*, Montreal *Gazette*, and Winnipeg *Tribune*, which last presented him with a gargoyle from their building. Also, he was former editor-in-chief of the Vancouver *Province*.

Charles Lynch, war correspondent for Southam Newspapers, is here interviewing wounded rifleman A. Jesson of the Winnipeg Rifles at Carpiquet. He became head of the Southam News Services and now, with his mouth-organ, has become popular as an after-dinner speaker.

Veteran news photographer Eddie Worth, with Associated Press, London, became attached to the Canadians in Normandy and worked with them in most of their actions. Now happily retired in Kent, he keeps fit working his land at 'The Oaks.'

THE ROAD TO FALAISE

After Caen, the next task of the British and Canadians was to fight their way towards Falaise, maintaining close contact with the enemy and keeping Panzer divisions tied up in front of the 2nd British Army, under Gen. Dempsey, the 1st Canadian Army now under Gen. Crerar, with the 2nd Canadian Corps under Lt-Gen. Simonds. The plan was designed to allow the Americans to break out in the west, while we continued to force the German towards Paris and the Seine. As expected, the Germans brought to the front the 9th and the 2nd SS Panzer Divisions, moving by night and hiding by day from our Tactical Air Force, along with the 116th Panzer Division from the Pas de Calais. This was grim news for the men fighting south of Caen, but good news for those planning the break-out by US troops.

The road from Caen ran in a straight line for 21 miles, gradually rising to a height of 200 metres north of Falaise at Potigny. The rolling countryside was covered in wheat, ideal for hiding defensive troops. At this time, the Germans introduced their Heavy Tank battalions, with the new 60-ton Tiger tank carrying the feared dual-purpose 88-mm gun. Dug in, these tanks were almost invulnerable, with 7-inch armour protecting their front. Their range and armour-piercing capabilities stunned our Shermans as quickly as they came into sight, and sometimes scores of Allied tanks were destroyed in a single engagement by the Tigers.

'Operation Spring' was the name chosen for the Canadian action in these beautiful but deadly Norman fields. The main attack, slated for 25 July, had the 2nd and 3rd Canadian divisions moving once again towards May-sur-Orne, St André-sur-Orne, St Martin-de-Fontenay, Rocquancourt, Bourgérthoulde, and the formidable Verrières Ridge. The entrenched Germans were ready, and the action became a blood-bath. To make matters worse, this was a mining area honeycombed with underground tunnels from which the Germans could pop up like groundhogs in the rear of the advancing troops and fire at will, disappearing only to reappear somewhere else. Besides being effective, with troops so easy to pick off from the rear, this frustrating action eroded Allied morale.

Gen. Simonds devised the use of artificial moonlight by bouncing searchlights off the clouds to give the army an extra boost in an early morning attack. H-hour was 3:30 AM, but the 'moonlight' backfired when it silhouetted our own troops for the enemy and they opened fire.

The Royal Regiment of Canada advancing on Rocquancourt ran into a murderous barrage from enemy tanks, and C Company was wiped out. After a deadly struggle, the Royal Hamilton Light Infantry made it to the top of Verrières Ridge under Lt-Col. Rock-

ingham, but the Black Watch paid dearly for their efforts at the ridge, losing 307 men. Rockingham's position was overrun by tanks, and the RHLI suffered 200 casualties; however, they somehow managed to hold, and by evening, rocket Typhoons broke up a counter-attack and most likely saved Verrières. 'Operation Spring' was called off. Up against a determined, experienced enemy, 450 Canadians had died, among more than 1,100 casualties, the bloodiest day for Canadians since the landings.

That same day, the Americans break-out 'Operation Cobra' commenced with 1,500 Flying Fortresses blasting the German defence. By 28 July, the US troops were in Coutances, and two days later they had pushed forward to Avranches. By now, the famous 3rd Army of Gen. George Patton was forming a left hook, while the 1st US Army continued pressure on Gen. Hausser's Germans on the right. At this stage, Hitler made the fatal decision to gather most of his Panzer divisions to hurl at the Americans at Mortain and Avranches, thus splitting the Americans up for piecemeal destruction. This went counter to the decision reached by von Kluge and his generals, but who was going to argue with Hitler? The attack duly began the night of 6 August, but the Americans, with strong support from the Allied Tactical Air Force, stopped the Panzer armour in its tracks.

Because of the Fuehrer's poor strategy, some of the best Panzer units were now in a position to be trapped in the pocket between Alençon and Falaise by Gen. Patton's left hook to the east. With the 51st Highland Division, the Polish Armoured Division, and a British armoured brigade joining 2nd Canadian Corps, Gen. Simonds made plans for a Canadian break-out to take Falaise, link up with the Americans, and trap the German 7th Army. He devised the idea of removing the guns, no longer needed, from the turrets of the 'Priests' of the self-propelled regiments and converting them into armoured troop carriers, thus creating the 'Kangaroo.'

General Simonds' preparations took time, and he could not begin until 8 August. The day before, troops and armour for this all-out attack were moving into position on the battle-scarred ground before Verrières Ridge. At 11:00 AM, 1,000 bombers roared overhead, dropping thousands of tons of bombs on the enemy positions. By 11:30, chaos reigned, as advancing columns lost their way in the heavy smoke and clouds of dust. Troops strayed from their target and many men were put out of action by the well-hidden Germans. By noon, the Canadians were reaching some of their objectives, but they became stalled later in the day and finally broke down. Shortly after noon, planes from the US 8th Air Force bombed Canadian and Polish positions, knocking out Divisional Headquarters and badly wounding Gen. Keller. More than 400 Polish and Canadian men were casualties.

By 12 August Gen. Patton's armour had reached Argentan, only 15 miles south of Falaise. The swashbuckling Patton wanted to continue onward and push the Germans into the sea to show his contempt for Montgomery, but Bradley and Eisenhower, fearing the worst if the boundary between British and American Army groups was ignored, convinced the General his glory lay elsewhere. Leaving some of his army to hold their positions, Patton took his pearl-handled pistols and the rest of his men to head towards the Seine and Paris.

On 14 August, 'Operation Tractable' began with Gen. Simonds calling for the support of the RAF, heavy bombers, and every gun in the army. The fields were massed with tanks, flails blowing mines in front of the advancing columns, as the action slowly began to move through the wheat fields in front of Quesnay Wood. Almost 1,000 bombers of Bomber Command blasted the enemy with 4,000 tons of explosives; unfortunately, yet once again, many of the bombers mistakenly unloaded on Canadian and Polish troops when the recognition signal proved to be the same colour as the target signal. By 16 August, with casualties mounting, Simonds sent the 2nd Division with armoured support to take Falaise, and the 4th Armoured Division and the Polish Armoured Division were to close the Gap and make contact with the Americans.

Occupying Falaise was the armour of the Sherbrooke Fusiliers and Le Régiment de Mont Royal. To the east, the newly indoctrinated armoured divisions were in a bitter life-and-death struggle with the cream of the German armies. At St Lambert-sur-Dives, a historic battle was being fought by a squadron of the South Alberta Regiment and a company of the Argyll and Sutherland Highlanders from Hamilton. The fighting was unbelievably brutal as the Germans tried to break through during the 19th and 20th of August, but the Canadians prevailed, killing many of the enemy and preventing thousands from escaping the Allied trap. For his heroic action at St Lambert, Maj. Dave Currie was to be awarded the first Victoria Cross of the northwest European campaign.

Soldiers are silhouetted against searchlights which create artificial moonglow for the move towards Falaise.

Battleworn veterans of D-Day cross the Orne in an outflanking manoeuvre to capture the Caen industrial suburbs of Vaucelles and Colombelles and open the road to Falaise. Pte Herman Geroux leads the HLIC Bren carrier across the Orne.
Inset Today he is a strong supporter of the Royal Canadian Legion at his home in Vancouver.

The three Geroux brothers, Herman, Harvey, and Art, were all in the Highland Light Infantry from D-Day to the victorious end, taking only hospital time-out, with a total of six wounds among them.

Royal Canadian Engineers, mine-clearing experts, often had to perform their tasks under fire. Here Spr C.W. Stevens of 18 Field Company uses a mirror to locate igniters under a German Teller Mine, which is then blown up. Another section keeps a wary eye open for snipers, as it sweeps the verges to allow military vehicles to advance again.

Vehicles of the 3rd CID move forward on the rich, rolling plains leading to Falaise, south of Vaucelles.

Below The thunderous roar of guns shatters the early morning air as troops wait for the firing to lift.

Plough your field
So richly fed.
It was courage here,
Freely bled ...
– Sydney Banks

Seasoned German troops, supported by huge Tiger tanks and 88-mm guns, provided stiff opposition to the Canadians. The going was slow and tough, the casualties mounted.

There are no heroes, only the survivors.

Top left Field Marshal Erwin Rommel, the magnetic leader of the Germans in the field, fell into disfavour with Hitler after the bombing in Hitler's bunker HQ in Berlin.

Flail tanks blow land-mines ahead of the advancing infantry.

For the benefit of the burial squads, the Canadian dead are marked by inverted rifles, mute reminders of the terrible cost of war.

Father LeNormand appears after the battle passes through Rocquancourt to assess the damages to his ruined church. Later, in the rebuilt church, schoolchildren pass under the watchful eye of their teacher.

A tired infantryman watches and waits.

A hunter seeks and stalks.

The village of May-sur-Orne on the road to Falaise is taken by Les Fusiliers de Mont-Royal after it was almost completely destroyed in bitter fighting.

On 8 August, Canadians were accidentally bombed by American planes at their headquarters in Cormelles, resulting in casualties and the destruction of equipment and supplies.

On 14 August, Canadians and Polish troops were hit again near Cintheaux by RAF and RCAF heavy bombers, because of a mixup in recognition signals. Numerous casualties were sustained, particularly in the Polish Armoured Division, along with the destruction of equipment and the loss of many lives.

May-sur-Orne was completely rebuilt with an unusual modern church replacing the towered stone structure seen so often throughout Normandy.

Sheep now graze on the rich grass beneath the apple trees where the American bombs fell.

A boy and his dog laze quietly where once the earth was shattered by 1,000-pound bombs.

The battle escalated to an inferno, as the cream of the German
Panzer divisions dug in to prevent any further Canadian
advance.

The 5th Welsh Regiment moves relentlessly forward on the right flank of the Canadians.

Two brothers try to be soldiers with the world erupting around them.

A battered prisoner, stunned by the fury of the fight, is brought into the prisoners' cage.

The old fort guarding the entrance to Falaise is blasted with shells from Canadian tanks.

Climaxing a month's bitter fighting, Canadians made their way into the burning shell ... the gutted remains of Falaise.

This picturesque scene is dominated by the old fort, barely scarred by the gunfire from the tanks.

Inset The streets are rebuilt and market-day shoppers fill the town square.

Harsh, cruel, and relentless was this place called Falaise, and bitter house-to-house fighting took its toll.

Inset Now youths invade the streets of Falaise, war the furthest thing from their thoughts.

The dead lay where they have fallen, and
snipers wait at every corner.
Inset The streets of Falaise today.

It becomes kill or be killed, as sniper firing continues and casualties must be seen to beside the stone wall.

A bicycle replaces the Sherman tank and good neighbours meet to gossip unafraid.

Tanks and men continue their grim hunt for the enemy house to house, with bayonet and grenade at the ready.

Another wounded victim is carried out of the range of a sniper to have his wounds attended to.

With tanks and self-propelled anti-tank guns, Maj. Dave Currie of the South Alberta Regiment and a group of Argyll and Sutherland Highlanders fought their way into the village of St Lambert-sur-Dives, consolidated, and held on there for several days against savage day-and-night counterattacks, as the enemy tried to break out of the Falaise pocket. For this gallant effort, Maj. Currie received the Victoria Cross, the first Canadian so honoured in the northwest Europe campaign.

St Lambert-sur-Dives bears few traces of those days when it seemed the world had gone mad.

At home in Ottawa, Dave Currie has taken up oil-painting.

During the heroic struggle to hold St Lambert-sur-Dives, Film and Photo Unit cameraman Sgt Stollery, along with Lt Don Grant, recorded the action for history. Stollery received the MM and Grant the MC. Both men were wounded in the engagement.

Two of Sgt Stollery's photos from his CINE films: a view of the action and one of the German surrender.

The Polish Armoured Division felt the heaviest weight of the Germans while trying to break out of the Falaise pocket. For a time, the Poles were cut off from the rest of the 1st Canadian Army and had to be supplied with ammunition by air drops.

They managed to hold, and the gap was closed. Here Maj.-Gen. S. Maczek gives an account of events to Warcos Lionel Shapiro, Ralph Allen, and J.A.M. Cook.

The battle for Falaise is over. Transport, guns, and equipment move on through the shell of the town towards the Seine and a retreating German Army.

THE SEINE AND THE PAS DE CALAIS

When the battle-weary Polish Armoured Division entered Chambois on 19 August and met troops of the 1st US Army, the Falaise Gap was finally closed. However, the corridor to the Seine remained open, and many of Hitler's crack troops managed to escape northward, fighting their way out in an impressive rearguard action. The Allied air forces bombed and shelled the corridor for three furious days, and soon the roads were blocked with burning tanks and wagons, dead men, and horses. Many were killed and thousands of the enemy surrendered in this holocaust. On 21 August, an unearthly silence fell over the scene. The Germans had gone and the Battle of Normandy was over, after 10 weeks of some of the most bitter fighting the world had ever known.

By then, Gen. Patton and his 3rd US Army had made a dash to the Seine, and on 25 August, Gen. Jacques Leclerc's 2nd French Armoured Division entered the French capital. Paris was free, but much remained to be done in northern France. On 15 August, during the battle for Falaise and the Gap, the 7th US Army under Gen. A.M. Patch had landed on the Mediterranean coast of France. This force, including many men of the Free French Army and the Canadian-American Special Services Force, rolled up the valley of the Rhone, while, on 26 August, the Canadians took over from American forces who were holding the banks of the Seine at Elbeuf, where the Germans were making a last-ditch effort to prevent a river crossing.

The Canadian objective was Rouen, the beautiful capital of Normandy, situated on a hill at the top of a broad bend in the Seine. To the south lay the Forêt de la Londe, a densely wooded area, where the 2nd CID encountered an entrenched enemy and several days' intensive fighting. Only after heavy casualties on both sides did the Germans withdraw, on 29 August. In the meantime, the 3rd CID had forced a crossing of the Seine at Elbeuf, aided by Free French Maquis, and civilian and military traffic was flowing freely over a pontoon bridge rapidly set up by Canadian Engineers. Rouen and its splendid medieval cathedral were undamaged, and the Canadians entered the city to the cheers of grateful citizens.

The Germans, reeling from their losses, withdrew to the Channel ports: Le Havre, Calais, Boulogne, and Dunkirk. The British Army crossed the Somme on 31 August, and, joined by the Americans, reached Brussels on 3 September. The Canadians were naturally intent on taking Dieppe, and mounted 'Operation Fusilade,' an assault by land by the 2nd Canadian Infantry Division,

with regiments of the 1942 tragedy. The Germans wisely withdrew, leaving Dieppe undefended. The first to enter the town, the 8th Reconnaisance Regiment (14th Canadian Hussars), were greeted by wildly enthusiastic townspeople, many weeping for joy after so many years of German occupation. Ceremonies were held at the cemetery in honour of Canadians buried there, and a parade marched proudly through the town, with Gen. Crerar taking the salute from his victorious regiments.

The Canadians had fulfilled their pledge to return to Dieppe and the Allies now had another port facility, which was opened to shipping in early September. After a few days' rest, the next stop was Le Havre, where special Canadian units joined the 1st British Corps, the flails leading the infantry through minefields, followed by Canadian squadrons in 'Kangaroos' and soldiers using 'Crocodile' flame-throwers. By 12 September, Le Havre had fallen, and the 3rd CID, now under the command of Maj.-Gen. Dan Spry, had entered the Pas de Calais to take Boulogne, while the 2nd Division moved north from Dieppe into the area of Dunkirk.

Clearing the coastal area, the Canadians took site after site used for launching the V-1, the dreaded flying bomb which inflicted so much damage on London and southern England. A jet-propelled robot missile carrying a 2,000-pound warhead which exploded on landing, the 'buzz bomb' made no distinction among men, women, and children, and after the first V-1 landed 13 June 1944, 6,000 of them were ultimately to cross to the English coast. Although some 3,000 bombs were shot down, 6,000 people died from these lethal weapons, and at least 20,000 were injured. Now, finally, the reign of the V-1 was drawing to a close, although the Germans were unhappily able to use the new, noiseless V-2 from bases in Holland until late in March.

After some probing of the enemy's defences, the 2nd CID moved into Belgium, while positions around the port of Dunkirk were taken over by a brigade of the 51st Highland Division and the 1st Czechoslovakian Independent Armoured Brigade, both under the command of Gen. Crerar and 1st Canadian Army. After initial bombing by 700 aircraft of Bomber Command, the 3rd CID moved into an attack on Boulogne on 17 September, and sustained a week of brutal fighting, with many casualties, until the city surrendered on 22 September. Without pause, on 23 September, the 3rd CID moved to Calais, along with the 2nd Canadian Army Brigade. During the attack, both sides declared a 48-hour truce so that civilians could be evacuated. After this, the fighting was supposed to resume, but the Germans apparently enjoyed the truce so much that they had little desire for battle.

It was all over at Calais by October, with only 300 Allied casualties, and a yield of 7,000 prisoners. The 9th Brigade had already attacked the Cap Gris Nez gun batteries, closest point to England and the source of much shelling of the British coast. Here 1,600 Germans surrendered with little resistance. Now it was on to Belgium – in particular, the Scheldt River basin and the key port of Antwerp.

This 7 feet 3 inches tall German POW, searched by Pte J.W. Butler, was captured at Cap Gris Nez.

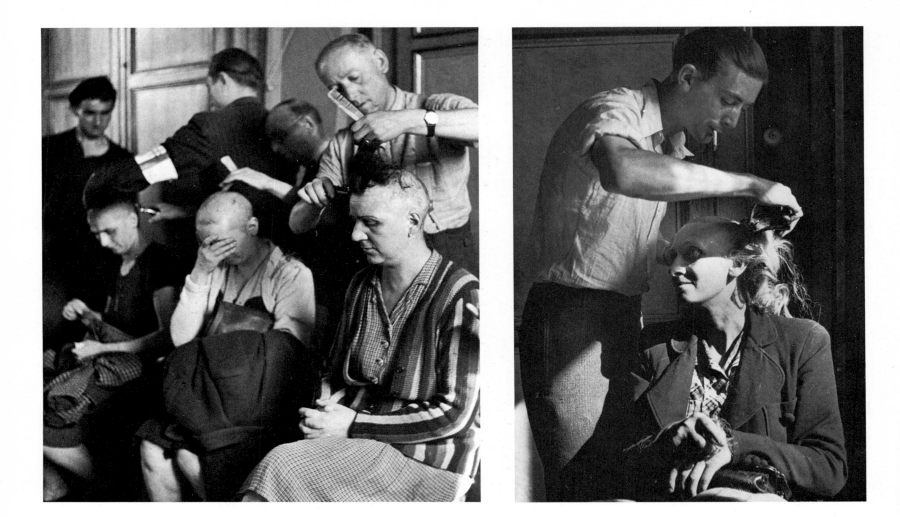

In the frenzy of liberation, suspected women collaborators were rounded up and their heads shaved. Then they were sent out on the streets, branded a friend of the Germans without a trial.

In the rapid advance towards the Seine, many prisoners were taken. Here a group of POWs is thoroughly searched by members of the Belgian brigade.

A British soldier and a member of the Maquis light up a 'fag' on the road to Abbeville and Amiens, names that still stir memories of the first great war.

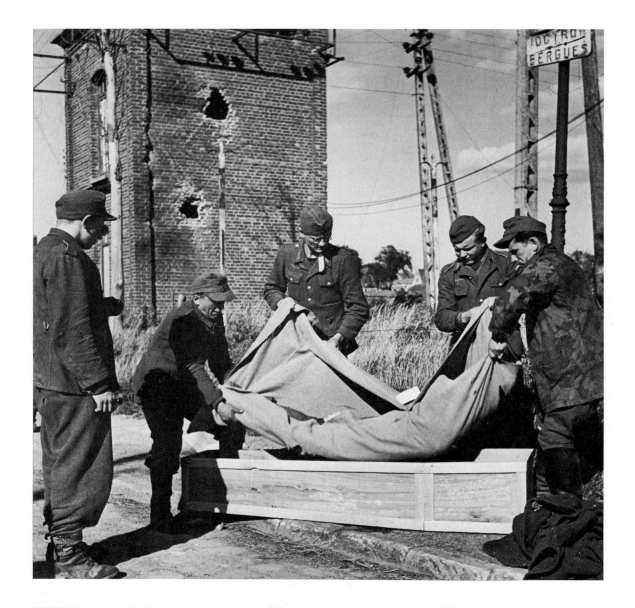

At the ancient walled town of Bergues, Maquis partisans put German prisoners to work burying the dead.

Schoolchildren accompany their teacher through the gate of Bergues.

Father fishes, as his son wonders if they're biting today.

L'Hôtel de la Corne d'Abondance in Bourgthéroulde was badly scarred in rearguard action from the retreating Germans. The divisional sign on the wall points the way to the Seine, and a Canadian Provost controls traffic at this busy crossroad.

Five years later the hotel has not changed much. Chef Lemay, who was hiding in the cellar while the battle went on, confers with a local gendarme.

25 years after the battle, the hotel has taken on a new look and young people gather at the corner to make plans.

Today the traffic is heavier, and this young lady has to sprint to cross the road.

In the British dash to the Seine, a Cromwell tank clears out enemy gun positions.

Royal Engineers build a pontoon bridge across the river.

Canadians reach the Seine at Elbeuf.

Prisoners pass a dead German, whose boots have been stolen.

Maquis round up prisoners in the hospital area.

At the Seine, Sgt B. Shaw admires the view. Above, decades later, the Seine still rolls serenely toward Rouen and the sea.

The teachers keep the children in order and warn about the
red light.

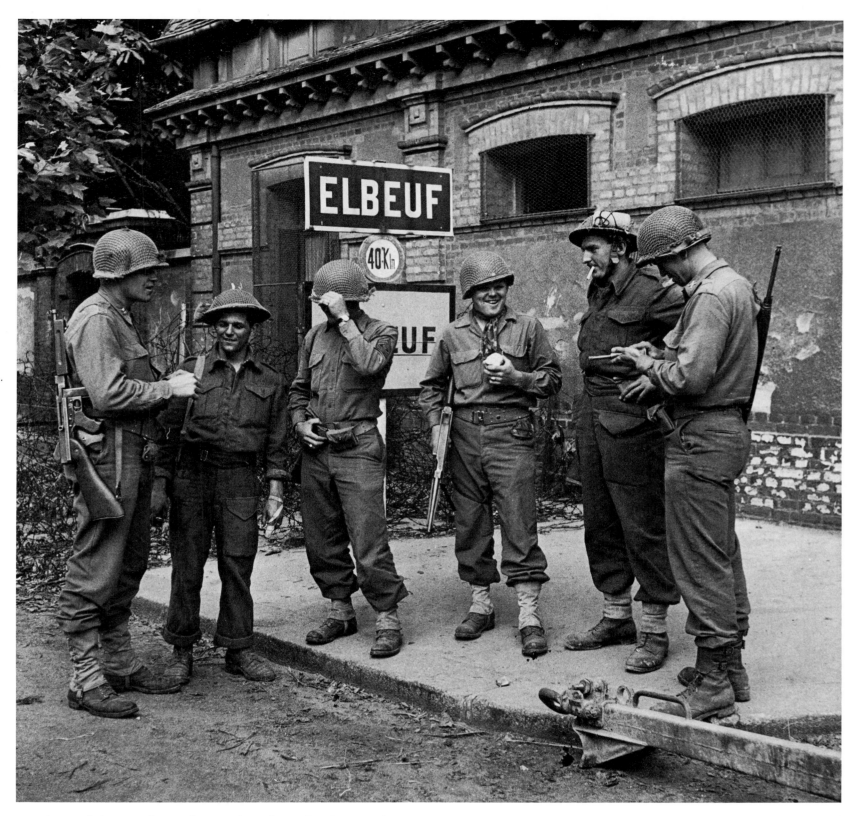

Members of the Royal Hamilton Light Infantry hook up with
the Americans at Elbeuf. After an exchange of cigarettes and
jokes, they move on to the task ahead.

In the early morning light, infantry moves across the Seine in rubber rafts, followed by vehicles on pontoon rafts.

Barges have regained control of the river, replacing military congestion.

The buildup was rapid, with pontoon bridges strung across the river, and the flow of traffic increased as the Allies pushed on towards Rouen against stiff enemy resistance.

A new bridge now spans the river and boys fish from the stone abutments of the destroyed bridge.

Germans enter Paris in June 1940 and parade past the Arc de Triomphe.

Paris is free. Gen. Charles de Gaulle approaches the Arc de Triomphe to lay flowers on the Tomb of the Unknown Soldier, 26 August 1944.

Gen. Leclerc watches the tanks of his division entering Paris on 25 August. The 1st US Army parades past the Arc de Triomphe, under which rests the Tomb of the Unknown Soldier.

Some are hit, others flee, during the indiscriminate firing.

The frenzied crowd in Place de la Concorde celebrates its liberation.

Today a photographer has his son pose in the almost deserted Place de la Concorde.

Paris again is a city of beauty and light.

The Hôtel de Ville and enthusiastic throngs on the Day of Liberation.

An abandoned German 88, one of the most feared guns in the war, now stands as if protecting the Canadian Bailey Bridge into Rouen.

The gun is long-gone, and schoolchildren pass where it once stood.

The Maquis were leaders in the liberation of Rouen, soon taking the town hall. Here they keep a watchful eye on the happenings in the square.

Three French soldiers stand in the square beneath the clock where partisans fought so bravely.

Enthusiastic crowds over-whelm Sgt Gordon Petty of the Film and Photo Unit.

The Maquis partisans had many veterans of the Spanish Civil War join their ranks, in-cluding this young girl with the cartridge-belt and rifle.

The people of Rouen keep up the sociable French tradition of visiting the outdoor cafés.

On the move to the Channel ports and Belgium, the Canadians took land which is truly a part of Canada itself, gallantly fought for. The magnificent Vimy Memorial commemorates the sacrifice of our fathers.

The 2nd Heavy Anti-Aircraft Regiment is bogged down in the mud of Dunkirk. With a lot of muscle and a winch, the gun is finally freed, to be used in containing the garrison in Dunkirk.

Many of the concrete gun emplacements have now been converted into homes with extremely thick walls and not too many windows.

The taking of the huge guns at Cap Gris Nez spelled the end of the bombardment on southeast England.

Multiple rockets are set up by the enemy in northern France while a soldier tucks into his sauerkraut and sausage.

Hundreds of prisoners are marched out of the rubble-filled streets of Boulogne. Two Germans, badly hit, are attended to by their medic. A very young soldier, a POW, tries to be a veteran by smoking an over-sized cigar.

The surrender at Boulogne yielded almost 10,000 prisoners, although our casualties were very high in taking this well-fortified town. Here prisoners are marching through town to POW cages. Senior officers surrender and Sgt B. Barnett, Film and Photo Unit, gets a few prisoners for himself.

Brig.-Gen. John M. Rockingham, Commander of 9 CIB which played a large part in the taking of Boulogne, received the DSO for this action. Later he commanded the Canadian Forces in Korea.
Inset Maj.-Gen. Rockingham in retirement at his home on Vancouver Island.

Field Marshal Sir Bernard Montgomery visits Gen. Crerar at 1st Canadian Army Tactical Headquarters.

The Russian Mission visits Gen. Miles Dempsey at 2nd British Army Tactical Headquarters.

Anthony Eden visits Gen. Crerar, escorted by Mary Churchill, his staff, and Scotland Yard.

Prince Bernhard of the Netherlands meets with Maj.-Gen. R. Urquhart, Commander 6th Airborne Division.

The Chinese Mission headed by General Sun Yat-sen visits the 1st Canadian Army in France.

King George VI arrives to visit the Armed Forces on the battlefield.

King George VI decorates Lt-Gen. Guy Simonds with the CBE at a ceremony near Antwerp.

BELGIUM AND
THE SCHELDT

While the Canadian Army was clearing the Channel ports and the Pas de Calais, elements of Gen. Dempsey's 2nd British Army, in a remarkable drive, had entered Antwerp on 4 September. On the previous day, other units had liberated Brussels. The Canadian 2nd Division and the 4th Armoured Division now gave up the static role of containing the Germans in Dunkirk and entered Belgium in early September with the task of clearing the coastal ports on the way to the Scheldt and Antwerp. Mikkelkerke and Ostende, with its huge U-boat pens, as well as Blankenberghe, were taken before the Canadians swung east towards Antwerp, liberating along the way such historic cities as Bruges, Eeklo, and Ghent on 9 and 11 September.

At this time, Field Marshal Montgomery was finishing his plans for 'Operation Market Garden,' a great airborne offensive to take the bridges in northwest Holland: the bridge at Grave over the Maas, the Nijmegen Bridge across the Waal, and the furthest objective, the Arnhem Bridge over the Neder Rijn. Montgomery felt that if it was successful and the armour could break out into the plains of Germany, the war would be over in 1944. The bridges over the Waal and the Maas were taken and held by the 82nd and 101st Airborne Divisions, but the 1st British Airborne was isolated at Arnhem when armour of the 2nd British Army failed to reach them, because of fierce German resistance beween Nijmegan and Arnhem.

With the failure of 'Market Garden,' the necessity of freeing the port of Antwerp grew even more desperate, as it seemed fairly certain there would be a long, hard winter campaign. With the supply lines stretched back to the beaches of Normandy, 1st Canadian Army and their attached Polish and British divisions were given the task of quickly clearing the Scheldt. The 2nd Canadian Division and the Polish Armoured Division moved to the east of Antwerp in an area along the Albert Canal. The 3rd Canadian Division, along with the 4th Armoured Division, now finished with the Channel ports, was to clear the area north of the Leopold Canal and the Canal de Dérivations de la Lys, which was held by excellent German troops in good defensive positions. In fact, the enemy controlled the whole area north to the Scheldt and from Braakman Inlet west to Knocke-sur-mer on the coast.

For the Scheldt campaign, the Canadian Army was to be commanded by Lt-Gen. Guy Simonds, replacing an ill Gen. Crerar who was temporarily returned to the United Kingdom, with Maj.-Gen. Foulkes taking over command of 2nd Canadian Corps and Brig. R.H. Keefler replacing Gen. Foulkes at 2nd Canadian Division. The clearing of the Scheldt was to become one of the most bitterly fought campaigns of the war, carried out under appalling conditions. Most of the flat land had been reclaimed from the sea. To keep sea-water out of the polders, the earth was criss-crossed by canals and dikes, which created ideal defensive positions for the resourceful enemy. None the less, by 22 September 2nd Division had forced a crossing over the Albert Canal and advanced to their next objective, the Antwerp-Turnhout Canal, along with the 49th British Division. After some very stiff opposition, they crossed the canal and by 22 October were well established in Merxen, north of Antwerp, a good base for the next phase: moving up to the entrance of the South Beveland peninsula.

Rapid progress was made until the Canadians neared South Beveland and the enemy threw in fresh battalions of paratroopers to stem the advance. Here, in the area of Woensdrecht, well-dug-in paratroopers calmly waited behind dikes as the Canadians moved across the flooded polders, only to be mowed down by withering enemy fire. Time and again, regiments of 2nd Division attempted to take the dikes and were caught in murderous cross-fire, many of the wounded drowning where they fell. Casualties were extremely high, reducing most regiments to less than half their strength; however, the men persisted heroically, and by 16 October, the Royal Hamilton Light Infantry had taken Woensdrecht and held it against furious enemy counter-attacks. By 23 October, the entrance to South Beveland was completely sealed off and the Canadians could start the job of clearing the enemy from the peninsula.

Meanwhile, 3rd Canadian Division on the south of the Scheldt was fighting another savage battle in flooded polders and dikes near the Leopold Canal. The enemy were so entrenched that it was decided to burn them out, and two dozen Wasp flame-throwers were brought up during darkness. In the early light of 6 October they opened fire on the enemy, while 7th Brigade, using assault boats, crossed the canal to gain a foothold on the far bank; however, the enemy counter-attacked so effectively that it was not possible to enlarge the bridgehead. On 9 October, 9th Brigade made a waterborne assault on the rear of the German position, sailing from Terneuzen across Braakman Inlet and landing on the south shore to ease some of the pressure at the Leopold Canal. Ferocious fighting continued for the rest of October and until the capture of Knocke-sur-mer on 3 November, when all resistance ceased. The south shore of the Scheldt was cleared of the enemy and Belgium became the first country in Europe to be completely liberated.

At the same time, 2nd Division was meeting equally stubborn resistance in its attempt to clear the isthmus and South Beveland. British 52nd Division launched an amphibious attack from Terneuzen across the Scheldt to land on South Beveland. This greatly aided the Canadians by splitting the German defenders, and South Beveland was cleared of the enemy by 31 October.

The only remaining obstacle to freeing the port of Antwerp was the capture of heavily defended Walcheren Island, linked to South Beveland by a narrow causeway. The plan called for two waterborne assaults and an attack across the causeway. Before the action, Gen. Simonds persisted in demanding that bomber command blow the dikes and flood the land to destroy German strong points, cut their supply lines, and allow Allied waterborne craft to move more freely. On 3 October, the RAF made a breach in the main dike at Westkapelle and on following missions enlarged the breach, which allowed the North Sea to flood the central portion of the island. Even so, German resistance was fierce and casualties were heavy, the British troops of 52nd Division and No. 4 Commando bearing the brunt of the fire.

By 8 November, the remaining enemy surrendered. At last, the Scheldt was free, and minesweepers began clearing the channels. On 28 November, the first liberty ship, the Canadian-built *Fort Cataraqui*, steamed into Antwerp harbour amid wild jubilation. In clearing the Scheldt, 1st Canadian Army had made a magnificent contribution. Obstinately the Canadians had outfought and outlasted a clever, powerful enemy under the most miserable of conditions, and their achievement in clearing the Scheldt should be long remembered.

The 2nd CID enters Belgium. Pte Hall talks to a happy gendarme at Nieuport.

The buzz bomb (V-1) had a frightening sound, and a devastating result when it landed. The 2nd Canadian Mobile Laundry and Bath all but disappeared after this bomb landed near Fort de Merxim.

Rightly called 'The Water Rats,' the Canadians along the coast and in the Low Countries seemed to spend more time in water than on land.

8th Recce Regt Anti-Tank crew protects the road to Dunkirk at the junction of Veurne.

A Vickers machine-gun firing as the 2nd CID starts to move north from Antwerp towards the Beveland Peninsula and Walcheren Island.

The roads are free of flooding and the water is back where it belongs – in ponds, creeks, and canals, ideal for fishermen.

18th Armoured Car Regiment takes a short stop in Blankenberge, so that petrol and supplies can catch up.

Men from the Royal Regiment of Canada take a break to rest their weary feet and light a cigarette.

Top A proud father walks his children across the street where warriors once stopped to rest.

On the sidewalk now, children play with their toy farm and herds of cattle.

André Vermuelen of St Croix on the outskirts of Bruges, member of the Underground 'White Brigade,' shows his hide-out under the living-room floor.

André's sister, Madeleine Vermuelen, in front of their home, L'Hermitage in St Croix.

Madeleine on Liberation Day looking at a bust of Hitler hanging in the town square with a Flemish placard saying 'The paper-hanger Fuehrer is finished.'

Madeleine and girl-friend Zette sit over the hide-out with the rug covering the trapdoor.

Top right Madeleine and Zette enjoying tea outside on the patio of the new 'Hermitage.'

Now Madeleine Nicod, she is standing at the same spot in the town square, but with the protective stone blocks removed from the monument.

Engineers clearing a heavily mined brick road leading into the critically important port of Antwerp.

Naval officers removing German Teller Mines from the harbour area.

British and American flags fly over Antwerp. In the excitement, the Union Jack was hoisted upside down.

The long-awaited first ship to pass through the Scheldt and enter
Antwerp was the Victory Ship SS *Cataraqui* on 28 November 1944.

One of the largest and finest harbours in the world, Antwerp sparkles
under the summer sun.

Dead bodies piled everywhere on the town square after a V-1 bomb landed during the noon-hour rush in Antwerp. The bomb probably was aimed at the harbour area a few hundred metres away.

The square today at noon.

Another view of the civilian massacre. Stunned people stand as though shell-shocked, while a few try to bring order to the confusion.

The same building, refurbished, stands in the background, and the street is crowded with prosperous citizens, many of them ignorant of the terrifying events that took place on this spot 44 years ago.

The Scout Platoon of the Calgary Highlanders, Cpl S. Kormendy sighting for Sgt H.A. Marshall, as they move out in front of their regiment.

The platoon moves cautiously towards Fort de Brasschaet, north of Antwerp, hoping to hold it as an observation post.

Personnel of the Royal Regiment fire a 3-inch mortar across
the Antwerp-Tornhout Canal north of Gravenwerel in Belgium.

Fort de Brasschaet is now a training and supply base for the
Belgian Army.

Boys fishing in the beautiful Belgian countryside.

On 16 December, von Rundstedt, hoping to retake Antwerp, launched a surprise winter offensive in the Ardennes against the 1st US Army. The enemy almost broke through American lines, but, against terrifying odds, the US held on tenaciously.

Bastogne was cut off and supplied by air drops. When asked to surrender, Gen. McAuliffe replied with the now-famous one-word message 'Nuts.' They stubbornly held until relieved by Gen. Patton and his 3rd US Army on 26 December.

Grimly and slowly the US 5th Army fought back and started to put pressure on the Germans.

McAuliffe Place, in the centre of Bastogne, is home to an American tank inscribed in memory of the brave men who prevailed here.

A carving at the end of a parkette in Bastogne pays tribute to Gen. Patton and the 3rd US Army.

HOLLAND

The 2nd British Army crossed into Holland on 12 September 1944 in the area of Eindhoven. After the airborne landings at Grave, Nijmegen, and Arnhem on 17 September, attempts by the 2nd British Army to reach the airborne at Arnhem were foiled by bad weather and a strong enemy. The gallant survivors of Arnhem were not to be withdrawn across the Neder Rijn until the night of 25 September. By the first week of October, Montgomery began to realize that this long, thin salient up through Holland, achieved at such high cost, was under constant pressure from the enemy and needed consolidation if the area was to be used as a base for future attacks into Germany.

First, a large pocket of resistance near Venlo on the Maas would have to be eliminated. The task was given to 7th US Armoured Division under command of British 8th Corps. Three days later, after very bitter fighting against a well-entrenched enemy protected by huge minefields, deadly 88s, and masses of artillery, not a yard of ground had been taken. After replacing the Armoured with the 3rd British Infantry Division, only slight headway was made and casualties were heavy. The Allies now at last understood that their hope for a quick victory in 1944 was gone and that it would be a hard winter's struggle against an enemy fighting desperately to save its homeland.

The US 1st Army did cross into Germany, however, and after stiff resistance managed to take the city of Aachen, although further moves into the valley of the Ruhr and an attempt on Cologne were beaten back. On 9 November, after its conquests in the Scheldt, 1st Canadian Army was moved to the Nijmegen bridgehead and set about to tidy up the salient and to clear the area between the Maas and the Neder Rijn, preparatory to any major break-out. Early in December, the Germans opened the dikes on the south side of the river and flooded large portions of already soggy ground, forcing the Canadians partially to withdraw. German paratroopers pursued, and only after a fierce battle and many casualties were they driven off. The 1st Canadian Army now became more or less immobile during the wet winter months, with constant patrolling and minor clashes here and there, as it continued to build up strength for the coming offensive into Germany.

It was during this period that Hitler once again took over the role of strategist. As commander-in-chief of the German Army, he made the decision to attack the Americans' loosely held positions in the Ardennes and strike for the port of Antwerp, thus splitting the British Army and creating another Dunkirk through Holland. He made his move on a bitterly cold day, 16 December, and the Americans did not expect the attack. Many storm-troopers

had quietly infiltrated the American lines the night before. As daylight broke, a barrage of 2,000 guns, the largest laid down by the Germans in the campaign, was hurled at the American divisions, as the German 5th Panzer Army moved towards Bastogne and St Vith, and the 6th Panzer Army against Monschav and Malmedy.

The Americans, taken completely by surprise, gave ground but did not break. Field Marshal Montgomery reacted quickly to the danger for Antwerp and moved his 30th Corps to the south, covering the road to Brussels and securing a line on the River Meuse. Although starting with a matchless tactical advantage, the Germans were held; while at Bastogne, completely surrounded, the 101st Airborne Division refused to surrender and were relieved on 26 December by Gen. Patton's newly arrived 3rd US Army. Soon the Germans had given up the initiative and the Americans recouped their losses. Again, Hitler's strategy had backfired, resulting in the loss of many crack divisions which would have been better used later on in defending the fatherland.

The gigantic offensive called the Battle of the Rhineland commenced early in the morning, 8 February 1945, and the 1st Canadian Army, strengthened by most divisions of the 2nd British Army and well supported by Allied air-power, found itself slogging through a quagmire of mud churned up by the weight of tanks and guns. The US 9th Army under Gen. Simpson was to attack the enemy and draw off German divisions from the Canadian front, but the Germans opened the dams of the Roer River, flooding ground the Americans had to cross. Instead of drawing off divisions from the Canadian front, they were able to withdraw some from the American front in an attempt to hold 1st Canadian Army, since the US 9th Army could not get going until 23 February.

With the arrival from Italy of 1st Canadian Corps, and a reunion with 2nd Canadian Corps after the Rhine crossing, the 1st Canadian Army had a right to be called truly Canadian. While driving north, the 2nd Canadian Corps re-entered the Netherlands to be greeted by ecstatic Hollanders – quite unlike the silent German people who had to watch the Allies fight through and destroy their towns. Maj.-Gen. Vokes' 4th Armoured Division crossed the Twente Canal, and by 5 April it had taken the town of Almelo. In spite of heavy shelling and constant counter-attacks the Canadians pushed deeper into Holland. After two days' hard fighting, the North Shore Regiment and the Régiment de la Chaudière cleared the historic town of Zutphen. Other elements of 3rd Division crossed the Ijssel River in assault boats, cleared the area, and continued their swift advance northwards, a move reminiscent of the exhilarating dash across northern France after the closing of the Falaise Gap.

In one week, 2nd Division advanced almost seventy miles to Groningen, the main industrial city of the north; after severe house-to-house fighting the city was cleared of the enemy. Third Division on 10 April captured Deventer, and a few days later Zwolle was taken. On 15 April the Royal Canadian Dragoons reached the North Sea at Zoutkamp and set up their headquarters in Leeuwarden with the happy approval of the Dutch. Northeast Holland was free, and now Gen. Foulkes and his 1st Corps, with the 49th British Division under command, began to clear Arnhem by forming a bridgehead across the Ijssel and launching an attack from the east. After two days, on 14 April, what was left of Arnhem was taken.

The Canadian 1st Division, freshly arrived from the Italian campaign, began a westward drive to take the important road and rail centre of Apeldoorn. At the same time, Gen. Hoffmeister and his 5th Armoured Division made a bold dash to the Ijsselmeer (the Zuider Zee), cutting off the German troops in Apeldoorn, who allowed 1st Division to take the city on 17 April. The Germans in western Holland were now separated from the main German army and set up a stout defensive line anchored on a series of waterways running through Amersfoort. Gen. Blaskowitz had 120,000 troops still holding western Holland, so rather than withdraw more troops from the front in Germany, the Canadians decided on a holding action and troops were ordered not to fire unless attacked. A truce was declared because of the food shortage, and immediately bombers started dropping rations to the starving citizens. By 1 May, food was being brought in by army trucks at the rate of 1,000 tons a day and deposited at a depot behind German lines for distribution by the Dutch authorities.

In the east, the German armies were beginning to collapse, and on 5 May, Gen. Blaskowitz surrendered the 25th Army in Holland to Gen. Foulkes in a hotel in the small town of Wageningen. The war was over for the Canadians, exactly 11 months after they had sailed from England to land on the beaches of Normandy.

Pte D. Tillick, Toronto Scottish, and Lt T.L. Hoy, Calgary Highlanders, wounded on the Beveland causeway, wait to have their wounds dressed at 18th Field Ambulance CCP, 1 November 1944.

The water-soaked earth of Beveland squelched under the weight of the Sherman tanks of the Fort Garry Horse, with anti-glider stakes planted in the flooded polders. There was no fear of enemy aircraft since the Allies now had complete control of the air.

German POWs are put to work carrying logs to cross the Beveland Canal so the armour can move forward toward Walcheren.

Tank-destroyer Shermans rumble over the flat countryside of Zeeland, making a tantalizing target for German 88s.

The signposts are still in place, as a Dutch family on bicycles crosses the new highway on the green light.

A smoke-screen is laid for an amphibious attack on Walcheren.

The marshy ground is hardly suitable for burials.

Casualties brought back across the Scheldt to Breskins.

Black Watch pipers play for 55 dead from a single company.

A pontoon raft takes tanks across the Beveland Canal.

An amphibious 'Alligator' carries men to Walcheren.

Soldiers fight on the banks of a canal.

Boys pick wildflowers where soldiers fought.

Animals killed by shellfire are soon butchered by the starving Dutch.

The cattle are well-fed and rich in milk.

Zeelanders stoically watch the military traffic pass.

Children play with model games on the sidewalk.

Alligators headed for Walcheren carry the North Shore Regiment off Breskins.

Pontoon rafts ferry vehicles over the canal while engineers work strenuously to complete a pontoon bridge.

Once the Germans blew the dikes, water became an enemy agent, impeding the advance.

The shallow waters of the Zuider Zee are ideal for windsurfing at sunset or by moonlight.

The flooded polders with their anti-glider stakes made large areas of Beveland impassable.
Inset With the water under control, fishing conditions are ideal.

Members of the Toronto Scottish Regiment borrow a local motorboat to make the crossing.
Inset A young boy rows his own boat on a Dutch canal.

Top Nijmegen became centre of the buildup of men and material for the early spring offensive.
Inset The same busy intersection as it appears today.

The destroyed bridge over the Beveland Canal. The engineers have quickly thrown a pontoon bridge across the waterway.
Inset Boys now fish where the enemy once dug in against advancing Canadians.

Most of the dikes formed ideal defensive positions, lined with shallow slit trenches – many later found with the bodies of dead Germans sprawled inside.

British Vickers machine-guns, perfect for this flat terrain, fire to break up a counter-attack.

The flooded ground bogged down much of the advance.

A German prisoner at a Canadian First Aid Centre gets a tetanus shot.

In an effort to end the war in 1944, Montgomery set up 'Operation Market Garden' to take the three bridges over the Waal, the Maas, and the Neder Rijn, using the 101st and 82nd US Airborne Divisions and the British 1st Airborne Division, with the Polish Airborne Regiment.

On 17 September, the bridges at Grave and Nijmegen were captured intact, but Arnhem on the Neder Rijn was 'one bridge too far' and the Germans held.

After the battle of the Scheldt, the Canadians took over the Nijmegen Bridge and the territory north towards Arhem across the Waal.

The renovated Nijmegen Bridge, a handsome sight in the glow of sunset.

Paratroopers of the 1st British Airborne fight on grimly even though surrounded by the enemy. Remnants of the division were withdrawn across the river in assault boats on 25 and 26 September. Many of the boats were manned by Canadian Engineers.

The Germans, masters at demolition, showed their expertise with the Arnhem bridge.

This idyllic spot, where a woman feeds the birds, is just across Arnhem Bridge.

The bridge has been replaced and fat cattle graze in its shadow; children flash a V for Victory.

On 5 April 1945, troops of C Company, North Shore Regiment, cross the Ijssel River at Zutphen against heavy sniper fire. One man has been hit. Le Régiment de la Chaudière uses rubber rafts to cross the river.

Five years following the war a new bridge, named 'Canadians' Bridge,' was built, with a commemorative plaque.

This couple from Zutphen crossing Canadians' Bridge has found an innovative way of reading a book. The bridge is a focal point of activity and enjoyment for the entire area.

Storm boats are manoeuvred into the Ems river by engineers of 3 CID.

Gunners of 4th Light Anti-Aircraft Regiment man their Bofors and watch the burning of a German ammunition dump north of Zutphen.

A windsurfing club was formed at the Ijssel River. Here young enthusiasts try to get the hang of it.

The Canadian troops from Italy were moved to northwest Europe to become a part of the First Canadian Army. Here the Princess Patricia Canadian Light Infantry disembarks from a 'Buffalo,' an amphibious vehicle used to cross the Ijssel River on 11 April 1945.

The Germans were still fighting a desperate rearguard action. Infantry of the South Saskatchewan Regiment fire through a hedge as the enemy makes a stand at the Oranje Canal.

Local children now play games in the sandbox.

Men of the Fusiliers de Mont Royal flush out prisoners on this street in Groningen, North Holland, as buildings burn furiously from shellfire.

People of Groningen stroll by the same location, unmindful of the drama that took place here so long ago.

GERMANY

The Allied operation to clear the area west of the Rhine, preparatory to the crossing, was code-named 'Veritable.' It was launched from the Nijmegen area between the Rhine and the Maas, and the 1st Canadian Army played a major role. Over the relatively quiet winter, the buildup of men and materials had been staggering, and Gen. Crerar's force was strengthened to 13 divisions, including 9 British divisions. More than 1,000 guns, the 1st Canadian Rocket Unit, thousands of tanks and mortars – indeed, almost every offensive weapon in the army's arsenal – were utilized, as well as the support of over 1,000 planes of the RAF Bomber Command and over 1,000 fighters of the 2nd Tactical Air Force. All that could be done was done, and the attack was to commence on 8 February.

During the night, heavy bombers had destroyed the towns of Goch, Udem, Cleve, and Calcar behind the Reichswald Forest. At five in the morning the thunderous roar of 1,000 guns opening fire shook the air as they hurled 160,000 shells into the enemy's defensive positions. By 10:30 AM the infantry started to move forward through the minefields on a six-mile front with five divisions: 2nd Canadian, 15th Scottish, 53rd Welsh, 51st Highland, and 3rd Canadian with a later start-time on the extreme north. The advance progressed well in the initial stages, but as the enemy recovered from the bombardment, so did their resistance, and the soft, wet ground hopelessly bogged down many Allied vehicles, causing traffic problems and delay. The 3rd Division cleared the flooded area between the Waal and the Nijmegen-Cleve road with amphibious vehicles, the 'Buffaloes' and 'Weasels.'

By the end of the first day, the advance had crossed the border into Germany, against sturdy resistance. However, the first of three German lines was now broken and the next objective was the formidable Siegfried Line, anchored on the Reichswald Forest, with every conceivable anti-tank ditch, land-mine, concrete fortification, and trip-wire for defence. At this stage, the enemy was throwing in all its available reserves, and it took five days of bitter fighting before the Reichswald was cleared, with casualties everywhere. During this time, the Highland Division took Gennep while the Scottish Division captured what the bombers had left of Cleve. Canadians were now involved in some of the bloodiest fighting of the war, trying to win the Goch-Calcar road as the Germans poured in fresh troops and units of the superb Panzer Lehr Division. By 21 February, 2nd Division had outfought the enemy and taken its objectives after terrible losses on both sides.

The last line of German defence before the Rhine included the town of Xanten and the heavily defended Hochwald Forest. On 26 February, Gen. Simonds launched his attack with 2nd Canadian Corps on the Hochwald; in the meantime, Gen. Simpson's 9th US Army, which had been held up by the flooding of the Roer Dam, had started its offensive on 23 February. The Germans were slowly being caught in a pincer movement between 1st Canadian Army and 9th US Army. Unfortunately for the enemy, they now had to move forces from the Panzer Lehr and 15th Panzer Grenadier Division in an attempt to stem Gen. Simpson's advance towards the Ruhr at Düsseldorf, even as the 1st US Army was approaching Cologne.

The attack on the Hochwald commenced on 1 March against impressive opposition from the German dug-in positions. Here Maj. F. Tilston with his company of Essex Scottish crossed open ground and barbed wire through a curtain of gunfire to gain a foothold at the edge of the forest. Maj. Tilston was wounded in the head, but, expertly firing his Sten gun, was the first to reach the enemy position. Leading his men to the German second line he was hit again, yet still managed to reorganize his depleted company against counter-attacks. Going for ammunition, he was wounded for the third time and turned over the remaining company to the only surviving officer. For his outstanding bravery, he received the Victoria Cross.

The fighting continued at a frantic pace and the casualties implacably mounted as the 1st Canadian Army inched its way towards the Rhine. The town of Xanten won, the Canadians and British pushed on, taking strongholds and fortified positions until, by 10 March, after more than a month of steady combat, the remaining German forces pulled back across the river, leaving the west of the Rhine in Allied hands. The stage was now set for the crossing of the Rhine into the heart of Germany.

The Allied cause was helped immeasurably by the German failure to blow the Ludendorff Bridge at Remagen, which was taken intact, though heavily damaged, on 7 March by units of the 1st US Army. For 10 days the Americans pushed men and equipment over the bridge into an expanded bridgehead, until, on 17 March, the bridge collapsed, killing 26 Americans. By that time, pontoon bridges were operating across the Rhine, and the Americans continued their buildup as the Germans moved fresh divisions to this danger area, lessening the pressure on the Allies elsewhere.

On the morning of 24 March the crossing of the Rhine commenced with 3,000 aircraft and gliders overhead protected by 1,000 Allied fighter aircraft. The 1st Canadian Parachute Battalion with the 6th Airborne dropped in the area north of Wesel. The Highland Light Infantry were the first Canadians to cross the Rhine, using the amphibious Buffaloes in the area of Emmerich. Followed by other units, they met fierce hand-to-hand fighting in the bombed-out shell of what had once been Emmerich, but by 1 April the Canadian Engineers had a bridge across the Rhine.

With a huge pincer movement, the US 1st and 3rd Armies had encircled the Ruhr, the major source of German armament. At the same time, Russian troops were nearing Vienna. The Canadians were moving north over flooded land similar to the polders of Holland. By now, Hitler had killed himself in his secret bunker and it was only a matter of time. By 4 May, 3rd Canadian Division reached Emden and Aurich in the north, while 2nd Division took Oldenberg and the Polish Armoured Division passed through Bad Zwischenahn. With no defence line to fall back on and no fresh troops to throw into the battle, the German army began to disintegrate very quickly and the war was soon over. The surrender of the German forces was signed at Rheims on 7 May 1945.

A German paratrooper, a prisoner from the Hochwald Forest, is still defiant.

221

Upon entering Germany, caution is the watchword and every building is carefully checked out.

A German grave in the Hochwald Forest.

Provost Lance-Cpl B. Duoka guards prisoners digging rows of graves.

GIs head towards the Rhine as shells burst around them.

GIs on the run to clear out a tunnel.

The body of a German who committed suicide.

The Hochwald Forest today.

An M10 tank destroyer, a Sherman tank mounting a 17-pounder anti-tank gun, moves up through the forest to protect the 2nd CID advance.

The Hochwald Forest was infested by crack enemy paratroopers; every foot of ground was contested to the bitter death.

A wounded Cameron Highlander is helped back to a RAP by his buddies.

A wounded and bedraggled German NCO is marched away by a swashbuckling Canadian.

The street today is neat and clean as people make their way to work or market.

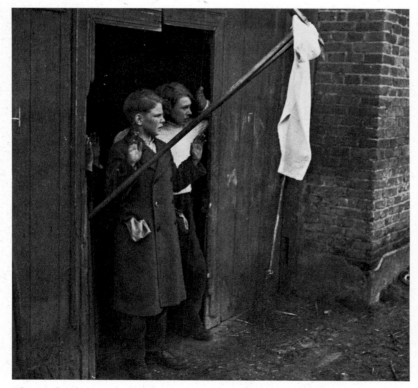

These frightened children came out with a flag of surrender as the Canadians swept through town.

There is no necessity for fear today.

These tough veterans of the Hochwald collect spoils of war: a few German hats and lots of worthless German marks.

The town square of Calcar, littered with debris.

In the square today anyone can enjoy an ice-cream.

Military traffic jams the rubble-filled streets of Calcar.

Young riders cross on their way to the stables.

The Staghound waits outside the medieval towers of Xanten.

228

The vehicles may change, but the twin towers have remained the same for centuries.

As a Company Commander with the Essex Scottish Regiment, Maj. Tilston led his men across open ground through barbed wire into the edge of the Hochwald Forest. Though wounded in the head, he pressed forward into the German second line of defence. With depleted troops he held on against counter-attacks and was hit again. He was awarded a richly deserved Victoria Cross.

The Canadian soldier, after vicious fighting in the Hochwald and on the west bank of the Rhine, gets a short break before the Rhine crossing. Involved in these carefree moments are men of the Queen's Own Camerons of Winnipeg, troopers of the Fort Garry Horse, and men of the Essex Scottish, including Pte J.A. Napier with top hat and cane and Pte A.V. Turner with a chicken under his arm.

3,000 aircraft and gliders crossed the Rhine on 24 March, giving a dazzling and encouraging show for the troops below.

Paratroopers, after landing across the Rhine, do a little mopping up ahead of the main forces.

Above After the crossing, Winston Churchill and Gen. H.D.G. Crerar, Field Marshal Viscount A.F. Alanbrooke, Lt-Gen. G.G. Simonds, and Field Marshal Montgomery gather on a high point overlooking the Rhine. In the background are Warcos Ross Munro and Charles Lynch.

A wounded soldier of the Stormont, Dundas and Glengarry Highlanders is brought back across the river for medical attention from the 9th CIB who were in the advance of the crossing.

On 7 March, US 9th Armoured Division captured intact the Remagen Bridge over the Rhine. It was one of the more fortunate incidents of the war, since demolition charges had been prepared but were not fired. On 17 March the bridge collapsed from the weight of traffic, killing 26 Americans and injuring 63 more. However, the bridge had done its job and the Americans were over the Rhine in great strength.

Inset The Ludendorff Bridge at Remagen. Only the towers were left after its collapse.

American GIs move German prisoners at the double to POW cages.

A 17-pounder anti-tank gun knocks the top off a high vantage point water-tower used by the enemy for observation.

As the battle moved into Germany, the full horror of war was brought home to the German people.

Refugees were everywhere, and the troops had little sympathy for them. Strategically located German snipers still caused damage at every canal or river crossing.

The 4th Canadian Armoured Division liberated a German POW camp on 12 April 1945 near Meppen, built for Russian prisoners from the Eastern Front. Here, pitiful inmates weigh their tiny allotment of food and dig in the garbage for any overlooked scraps.

VICTORY

There was happiness, there was jubilation, but there was also much sadness and many haunting memories. One had the time now to think and remember. The war had ended for the Canadians in Holland at the signing of the surrender of the German 25th Army by Gen. Blaskowitz to Lt-Gen. Foulkes at Wageningen on 5 May, and in Germany on the same day in Bad Zwischenahn, when Lt-Gen. Simonds accepted the surrender of Gen. Straube and his Army of the Northwest. On 7 May, the formal surrender took place on the heath of Luneburg, where Admiral Hans-Georg von Friedeburg as commander of the German Navy surrendered 600,000 men in Holland, Germany, and Denmark to Field Marshal Montgomery. In Italy, on 2 May, all German forces had surrendered to Field Marshal Alexander.

There was still the war against Japan in the East. On 6 August 1945, the first atomic bomb was dropped on Hiroshima and on 9 August a second bomb largely destroyed Nagasaki, ending the conflict in the Pacific. The nuclear age had begun, but there was rejoicing and relief as prisoners of war for many years were released from their camps of horror, many pitifully weak and semi-starved. The captured Russian POWs were in dreadful condition when freed by the Canadians, sick and emaciated, the bones showing through their skin, and fighting for scraps of food from the garbage piles. Even worse were the revelations of Belsen, Buchenwald, Dachau, and the other concentration camps with their obscene ovens and torture rooms, some preserved today as memorials to the victims, silent reminders of man's inhumanity to man.

The end of the war brought its shocks, but for most of those who had fought so long and so hard, it was time to relax and celebrate. Canadians, in particular, were lucky enough to enjoy the enthusiastic warmth of the grateful Dutch people. Parades were held throughout the cities and towns of Holland, flags flying from every building, as thousands of wildly cheering citizens threw flowers and kisses to the men of Canada's finest regiments. For Canadians, this was truly the memory of a lifetime. One of the largest parades was held in Amsterdam, where the troops proudly marching past were reviewed by Queen Wilhelmina as she stood on the balcony of the Royal Palace.

It was not all glory, for there was still work to be done, one major job being the evacuation of the German Army from Holland and its return to the homeland. The causeway on the Zuider Zee was to be the exit route, and it was a sad day for the once-mighty Wehrmacht when a long, straggling column of more than 100,000 men, with horse-drawn carts carrying stoves, bedding, and food, set out on the 300-mile journey back to defeated Germany. Gen. Foulkes had made it very clear that none of the loot stolen and plundered from across Europe was to leave Holland. He established search camps at several points, and millions of guilders, much jewellery, fine clothing, paintings, furs, and other valuables were discovered and redistributed to the people of Holland.

Canadian soldiers waiting for their own return home did their best to help out the Dutch in this busy time of reconstruction. Army engineers worked at draining the flooded polders, rebuilding bridges, and clearing canals, and many Canadian farm boys aided Dutch farmers in the fields, while still others cleared the shattered streets of the villages and towns. At the same time, the army was bringing in more than 3,000 tons of food a day for distribution throughout the Netherlands. It's no wonder that a warm friendship remains between the Dutch and the Canadians, as strong today as it was in those happy months following the end of the war – a friendship further cemented by the many marriages made between Canadian soldiers and the attractive girls of Holland.

All of this joy was not without its price. The returning men of the Canadian Armed Forces left behind, in the countries of Europe, in Hong Kong, and in the seas of the world, 42,000 comrades who would never come home. These men made the supreme sacrifice so that we who are here might enjoy a free world and a better life.

Remember them.

The people in Holland go wild at the miraculous news. At long last, the war in Europe is over!

Discussions about the surrender are held on a telephone linkup between Canadian and German Forces in Wageningen, Holland.

Even with surrender so near, the dead still need to be buried.

While surrender talks go on, Dutch collaborators are rounded up in their homes and on the streets.

The formal surrender of the German Army took place at Rheims on 7 May 1945 with Field Marshal Montgomery for the Allies and Field Marshal Wilhelm Keitel for the defeated Germans.

The German forces in northwestern Germany surrendered to Canadians in Oldenburg on 5 May 1945.

In a small hotel in Wageningen, Holland, Lt-Gen. Foulkes, GOC 1st Canadian Corps, dictates terms to Gen. Blaskowitz for surrender of all forces in the Netherlands, 5 May 1945.

The book of surrender is shown here on the same table and in the same room where it was signed. A pretty Dutch girl leans against the hotel wall where a plaque has been mounted to commemorate the signing.

Russian troops celebrate the end of the war by displaying an American flag.

Lt-Gen. Guy Simonds is the guest of Prince Bernhard and Princess Juliana at a Victory Ball.

Group of senior generals: *seated*, Field Marshal B. Montgomery, Gen. D.D. Eisenhower, and Lt-Gen. Omar Bradley; *standing*, Gen. H.D.G. Crerar, Lt-Gen. W.H. Simpson, and Lt-Gen. Sir Miles C. Dempsey in Hilversum, the Netherlands.

Lt-Gen. C. Foulkes, CB, CBE, DSO, GOC
1st Cdn Corps

Maj.-Gen. C. Vokes CBE, DSO, GOC
1st CID

Lt-Gen. E.L.M. Burns DSO, OBE, MC,
GOC 1st Cdn Corps

Brig. Gen. 'Jock' J.G. Spragge, DSO, OBE,
ED 7th CIB

Maj.-Gen. D.C. Spry DSO, GOC 3rd CID

Maj.-Gen. A.B. Matthews CBE, DSO, ED,
GOC 2nd CID

Group of generals of 1st Cdn Army at Hilversum 20 May 1945.
Seated: Maj.-Gen. H.S. Maczek, Lt-Gen. G.G. Simonds,
Gen. H.D.G. Crerar, Lt-Gen. Foulkes, Maj.-Gen. B.M. Hoffmeister.

Standing: Maj.-Gen. R.H. Keefler, Maj.-Gen. A.B. Matthews, Maj.-
Gen. H.W. Foster, Col. R.W. Moncel, Brig. Gen. S.B. Rawlins.

245

The Pipe Band of Canadian Women's Army Corps in Leeuwarden played for the troops from one end of Holland to the other, and in Germany and Belgium, led by Pipe-Major Lillian Grant of Victoria (*front left*).

Inset The Pipe-Major, now Mrs John Davis, revisits Leeuwarden, North Holland, 40 years later, enjoys a cup of tea, and reminisces.

The Victory Parade in Utrecht to celebrate the liberation of the Netherlands and the end of the war.

The triumphant hero Gen. Crerar returns to Halifax and is greeted on board ship by Gen. Andrew McNaughton, Minister of National Defence and Lt-Gen. J.C. Murchie, Chief of the General Staff.

Gen. Crerar disembarks to the cheers of the troops aboard, who display a Nazi flag back to front.

WAR PHOTOGRAPHERS

Gord Aikman, retired from the Winnipeg *Free Press*.

Gilbert Milne, portrait photographer, Toronto.

Don Grant, retired in Poole, England.

Alex Stirton, retired from the government, Hull, Quebec.

Harry Clements, senior bartender at the Long Bar, Toronto Sheraton.

Bud Roos, retired in Victoria, BC.

Al Grayston, left film work to carve figures of animals; Montreal.

Ken Bell, commercial photography, Toronto.

Bill Grant, retired, Gibsons, BC.

Lew Weekes, semi-retired in Vancouver.

Len Thompson, retired from Canadian Superior Oil, now in Victoria, BC.

Michael Spencer, president, Film Finances Canada, Montreal.

Brian O'Regan, a vice-president of Northern Telecom in Ottawa.

Graham Campbell, a leading illustrator in Toronto.

George Cooper, retired in Ottawa from a successful construction business.

Gord Petty, retired from the CBC Film Department.

Norm Quick, retired from the government to play golf, Ottawa.

Bob Campbell, now retired in Mississauga, Ontario.

Fred Steele, square dance champion from Kelowna, BC.

George Game, electrical construction business in California.

Charlie Ross, here with Maj.-Gen. C. Vokes, now in Edmonton, Alta.

Ernie DeGuire, runs a photo operation in Kemptville, Ontario.

Ted Pritchard, retired from the photo sales business.

Charlie Richer, now lives near San Diego, California.

Al Calder, in the antique business in Victoria, BC.

Frank Dubervill, from Ottawa, deceased.

Al Calder meets with a Russian combat photographer in Germany.

Burial of **Sgt Jimmy Campbell**, one of the photographers killed while recording the history of the war.

PICTURE CREDITS

All colour photographs by Ken Bell,
with the exception of three as listed

Code for credits
AP — Associated Press
CINE — Stills from War Film
DND — Department of National Defence
FRGA — Federal Republic of Germany
Archives
IWM — Imperial War Museum of Britain
NAA — National Archives of America
NAC & PA — National Archives of Canada
NFB — National Film Board of Canada

Code for positioning
T — Top
M — Middle
B — Bottom
L — Left
R — Right

1 NFB CINE
2 NAC, Ken Bell
11 FRGA
12 T&B: NAC (DND)
14 BL&BR: FRGA
15 FRGA
16 NAC (DND)
18 FRGA
19 NAC (DND)
20 FRGA
21 Inset: John Foote
22 T: NAC (DND)   B: NAC (DND) 39658,
Ken Bell
23 T: NAC PA 131232, Ken Bell
24 NAC PA 134448, Ken Bell
25 L: Clive Webster (colour)   B: unknown
27 NFB CINE
28 T&M: NFB CINE   B: NAC PA 141664
30 NAC (DND) 33125, A.M. Stirton
32 TL, ML, TR&MR: NFB CINE   BL: PA (DND)
C 37629   BR: PA (DND) C 37626
34 T: PA (DND) 22030, A.M. Stirton
B: PA 138269, Jack Smith
36 TR: PA (DND) 21786
37 PA 136216, T. Rowe   TR: PA 132779,
T. Rowe
38 PA 151547, A.M. Stirton
41 PA 141699, A.M. Stirton
42 T: PA 136218, D.E. Dolan
43 T&M: NAC, no numbers   B: PA 136303,
C.E. Nye
44 PA 144103, A.M. Stirton
47 T: PA 140842, Jack H. Smith   B: PA 114482,
A.M. Stirton
48 TL: NAA 111 SC 212978   TR: NAA 80
G 58431   BL: NAA 80 G 43153
BR: NFB CINE

49 All photos: NFB CINE
50 TL: PA 136199, J.H. Smith   TR: PA 136307,
J.H. Smith   BL: PA 129766, J.H. Smith
BR: PA 136195, J.H. Smith
52 T: PA 130617, A.M. Stirton   B: PA 136303,
C.E. Nye
53 T: PA 141671, T. Rowe   B: PA 129762,
C.E. Nye
55 T: PA 129779, J.H. Smith   B: DND 25463,
A.M. Stirton
56 T: DND CINE   BL: FRGA   BR: DND CINE
57 T: PA 141662, T. Rowe   B: CINE
58 TL: IWM NZ12810   TR: IWM NZ12812
B: IWM EA17886
59 TL: PA 144726, A.M. Stirton   TR: PA 136204,
W.H. Agnew
60 All photos: NFB CINE
62 All photos: NFB CINE
63 TL: NAC   TR: PA 141670, T. Rowe
BL: PA 141662   BR: PA 115190,
F. Whitcombe
64 T: PA 136308, T. Rowe   B: PA 136311,
S.E.E. Smith
66 T: PA 141698, B. Gilroy   B: PA 140208,
S.E.E. Smith
67 TL&BL: NAC
69 NAC, Ken Bell
70 Count du Monceau
71 T: NFB CINE   B: FRGA
72 T&B: NFB CINE
73 T&B: NFB CINE
74 All photos: DND CINE
76 TL, ML, BL, MR, BR: DND, NFB, CINE
TR: PA 138266 French photo
77 Ken Bell
78 T: IWM B 5218   B: IWM B 5114
79 T: IWM BU 1186   B: NAA 26G-2343
80 T: NAA 111-SC 190405   M: NAA 111-SC
190062   B: NAA 111-SC 189932-S
81 T: PA 131506, G.A. Milne
82 T: PA 133742, Ken Bell   B: PA 141676,
K. Bell
84 T: PA 128790, F.L. Dubervill   B: PA 133754,
F.L. Dubervill
85 T: PA 115544, F.L. Dubervill   B: PA 114493,
Ken Bell
86 T: DND 33779, F.L. Dubervill
87 T: PA 140848, Ken Bell
88 T: NAA 26-G 2517   B: NAA 111-C 320886
91 NAC (DND) 38096, Ken Bell
92 TL: PA 132852, Ken Bell   ML: DND CINE
BL: PA 129042, Don Grant   TR: DND CINE
MR&BR: FRGA
93 TL: PA 129037, Don Grant   BL: PA (DND)
34075, Ken Bell
94 All photos: DND NFB CINE
96 T: NAC, Ken Bell   B: PA 136207, Ken Bell
97 T: PA 115569, Ken Bell   B: PA 141715,
Don Grant
98 PA 133962, Ken Bell
99 PA 132807, Ken Bell
100 TL: PA 136042, Gord Aikman
BL: PA 131428, Ken Bell   TR: FRGA
BR: PA 132723, Ken Bell
101 TL: PA 137357, Ken Bell   BL: PA 140141,
Ken Bell   TR: PA 115087, Ken Bell
BR: PA 129031, Ken Bell
102 PA 135906, Ken Bell
103 PA 142265, Ken Bell
104 T: PA 132191, Ken Bell   B: NAC (DND)
36231, Gord Aikman

105 PA 129130, Ken Bell
106 TL: PA 137028, Ken Bell   TR: PA 137027,
Ken Bell   B: DND 39123, Ken Bell
108 T: PA 138272, Ken Bell   M: PA 133109,
Ken Bell   BL: PA 133117, Ken Bell
BR: PA 133116, Ken Bell
110 TL: IWM B 6318   TR: PA 131397, Ken Bell
111 TL: DND CINE   TR: IWM B 6000
BL: FRGA   BR: PA 140855, Ken Bell
112 T: PA 116544, Ken Bell   BL&BR: Ken Bell
114 PA 116545, Ken Bell
115 PA 132873, Ken Bell
117 PA 116510, Gord Aikman
118 T: PA 136219, Don Grant   BL: PA 138268,
Ken Bell   BR: NAC, Ken Bell
120 PA 135905, Ken Bell
121 TL: PA 138284, Ken Bell   BL: PA 139288,
Ken Bell   TR: PA 136313, Ken Bell
BR: PA 116290, Ken Bell
122 TL: PA 138275, Ken Bell   BL: PA 115029,
Ken Bell
123 PA 116543, Ken Bell
124 T: PA 114508, Ken Bell   BL: PA 135907,
Ken Bell
125 DND 28892, Ken Bell
126 DND 36392, Ken Bell
127 T: DND 36360, Ken Bell   B: DND 36494,
Ken Bell
128 TL: PA 131395, Ken Bell   BL: Unknown
TR: Count du Monceau (colour)
129 TR: PA 136206, Ken Bell   BM: PA 141705,
M.M. Dean   BL: Unknown
131 PA 140857, M.M. Dean
132 T: PA 136850, Ken Bell   B: Unknown
133 T: DND 35506, Ken Bell   BL: PA 136278,
Ken Bell   BR: PA 137307, Ken Bell
134 T: PA 116536, Don Grant   B: PA 116516,
Ken Bell
136 All photos: FRGA
137 T: PA 131397, Ken Bell   B: DND, Ken Bell
138 TL: FRGA   ML: NFB CINE   BL, TR&MR:
NFB CINE   BR: PA 141712, M.M. Dean
139 TL: PA 132962, Ken Bell   BL: DND 38411,
Ken Bell
140 T: PA 132961, Ken Bell   M: PA 132657,
Ken Bell   B: PA 131375, Ken Bell
142 T: DND 38315, Don Grant   B: PA 140878,
Ken Bell
143 DND 38087, Ken Bell
144 TL: IWM B 8959   TR: IWM B 8967
BL: PA 132724, Ken Bell   BR: PA 114495,
F.L. Dubervill
145 TL: NFB CINE   B: PA 132193, Ken Bell
146 T: PA 132719, Don Grant   B: PA 132192,
Don Grant
147 T: PA 136211, Don Grant   B: PA 132194,
Don Grant
148 T: PA 135908, Don Grant
149 T: PA 132822, Don Grant   B: PA 115567,
Don Grant
151 T: PA 111565, Don Grant   B: PA 140875,
F.L. Dubervill
152 T: PA 115571, Don Grant   BL&BR: NFB
CINE
153 T: PA 129140, Ken Bell   B: PA 145557,
Ken Bell
155 PA 133136, Don Grant
156 TL: PA 140861, Ken Bell   TR: DND 39258,
Ken Bell   B: PA 140853, Ken Bell

157 T: PA 141724, Ken Bell B: PA 131222, Ken Bell

158 T: PA 141718, Ken Bell B: DND 40377, Ken Bell

160 TL: DND 39302, Ken Bell TR: Ken Bell

161 T: IWM B 9712 B: IWM B 9717

162 TL: PA 138276, Ken Bell ML: PA 115861, Don Grant BL: M.E. Mallenquery – Maquis

163 PA 131223, Ken Bell

165 PA 131345, Ken Bell

166 TL: M.E. Mallenquery – Maquis TR: PA 135958, Ken Bell

167 TL: Eddie Worth (Associated Press) TR: PA 113662, Ken Bell

168 T: NAA 242-EB-7-41 B: PA 135911, F.L. Dubervill

169 TL: NAA 111SC 193235 TR: NAA 208 YE-68

170 T: PA 135912, F.L. Dubervill M: IWM BU 134 B: PA 142903, F.L. Dubervill

171 BR: PA 142903, F.L. Dubervill

172 PA 151553, Ken Bell

173 TL: DND 39498, Ken Bell TR: PA 141717, Ken Bell BL: NAC, Ken Bell

174 T: PA 137031, Ken Bell B: NAC, Ken Bell

175 BL: PA 140866, M.M. Dean

176 T: PA 151554, Ken Bell BR: PA 133139, Don Grant

177 TL, ML, & MR: FRGA TR: NAC, Don Grant BR: PA 137447, Ken Bell

178 TL: PA 136333, Don Grant ML: PA 141721 Don Grant BL: PA 140873, Don Grant

179 PA 136759, M.M. Dean

180 T: PA 140409, Ken Bell M: PA 136209, Ken Bell B: PA 136315, Ken Bell

181 TL: PA 141725, F.L. Dubervill BL: NAC, Ken Bell TR: DND 54282, Ken Bell BR: NAC, Ken Bell

183 PA 131225, Ken Bell

184 TL: PA 136322, Ken Bell TR: PA 116728, Ken Bell BL: PA 141720, Ken Bell BR: NFB CINE

186 T: PA 142904, Ken Bell M: PA 140862, Ken Bell B: PA 140864, Ken Bell

188 T: PA 145497, Ken Bell BL: Ken Bell BR: PA 140863, Ken Bell

189 TL: PA 145498, Ken Bell

190 T: NAC DND 41028, Ken Bell BL: PA 140854, Ken Bell BR: PA 137317, Ken Bell

191 T: PA 136790, Ken Bell

192 T: AP, Eddie Worth

193 T: AP, Eddie Worth

194 TL: PA 141722, Ken Bell TR: PA 141723, Ken Bell B: PA 116737, Ken Bell

195 T: PA 116745, Ken Bell

196 T: NAA 208 YE99 M: NAA 208AA 20285 B: NAA 208YE-107

199 PA 141727, Ken Bell

200 T: PA 138429, Ken Bell B: PA 140876, Ken Bell

201 NAC DND 42128, Ken Bell

202 TL: PA 141726, Don Grant ML: NFB CINE BL: PA 140874, Ken Bell TR: PA 137205, Ken Bell MR: PA 136810, Ken Bell BR: NFB CINE

203 TL: PA 113908, Don Grant ML: PA 129760, Ken Bell BL: PA 137917, Ken Bell

204 T: NAC (DND) 41561, Don Grant M: PA 145702, Colin McDougall B: PA 131257, Ken Bell

206 T: PA 140871, Ken Bell B: PA 138409, Ken Bell

207 T: PA 140880, Don Grant B: PA 138427, Ken Bell

208 T: PA 140870, Ken Bell B: IWM BU 11651

209 T: PA 131252, Don Grant B: NAC DND 42237, Ken Bell

210 IWM B10175

212 TL: IWM BU 1167 TR: IWM BU 1098

214 T: PA 130059, Don Grant BL: PA 133331, Don Grant BR: Ken Bell

216 T: PA 138285, Don Grant B: PA 138282, Don Grant

217 B: PA 133333, G.B. Gilroy

218 T: PA 138284, D. Guravitch

219 T: PA 130964, D. Guravitch

221 PA 129756, Ken Bell

222 T: NAC, Ken Bell BL: NAC, Ken Bell BR: PA 137450, Ken Bell

223 T: NAA 111 SC 205298 BL: NAA 306NT855-3 BR: NAA 111 SC 193562

224 B: NAC DND 47636, Ken Bell

225 T: NAC DND 47610, Ken Bell B: NAC DND 50810, D. Guravitch

226 TL: NAC DND 49708, A.M. Stirton BL: PA 113697, A.M. Stirton

227 NAC DND 47621, Ken Bell

228 TL: NAC DND 47184, Ken Bell ML: PA 137452, Ken Bell BL: NAC DND 47619, Ken Bell

229 Inset: PA 132827, M.M. Dean

230 TL: PA 137457, Ken Bell ML: NAC 47626, Ken Bell BL: PA 137456, Ken Bell TR: PA 137465, Ken Bell MR: PA 140885, Ken Bell BR: PA 141729, Ken Bell

231 TL: PA 137460, Ken Bell BL: PA 140881, Ken Bell TR: PA 137458, Ken Bell BR: PA 137459, Ken Bell

232 TL&TR: NFB CINE B: NAC DND 48607, Ken Bell

233 T: PA 143952, B.J. Gloster B: PA 140888, Don Grant

234 T: NAA 111 SC 33317 B: NAA 111 SC 1940608

235 T: PA 137312, Ken Bell ML: NAC DND 47196, Ken Bell MR: PA 138278, H.G. Aikman BL: PA 135913, Jack Smith BR: NFB CINE

236 TL: NAC DND 47156, Ken Bell TR: NAC DND 47633, Ken Bell BL: NAC DND, Jack Smith BR: PA 129752, A.M. Stirton

237 TL: PA 132592, A.M. Stirton TM: PA 142905, A.M. Stirton TR: PA 132598, A.M. Stirton M: PA 142907, A.M. Stirton B: PA 142906, A.M. Stirton

239 PA 133153, A.M. Stirton

240 T: PA 134408, J.E. DeGuire B: NAC, B.J. Closter

241 TL: PA 140887, M.M. Dean TR: PA 137042 BL: NAC DND 49148, M.M. Dean BR: NAC DND

242 TL: IWM BU 5207 TR: NAA 306 NT 1342 B-3 BL: NAC DND 51586

243 PA 138588, A.M. Stirton

244 T: PA 136329, F.L. Dubervill M: NAC 59386, Ken Bell B: PA 136327, B.J. Gloster

245 TL: PA 133972, J.H. Smith TM: NAC TR PA 115498 C.E. Nye ML: PA 132816, Don Grant MM: PA 137029, Don Grant MR: PA 138399, Ken Bell B: PA 134281, Ken Bell

246 T: PA 141730, M. Angelo B: NAC 53985, Ken Bell

247 T: PA 145492, Ken Bell B: PA 145491, Ken Bell

248 TL: Gord Aikman ML: F. Dubervill BL: Don Grant TR: RCN Photo MR: A.M. Stirton BR: F. Dubervill

249 TM: Don Grant MM: Eddie Worth BM: F. Dubervill MR: George Hunter (colour)

250 TL: Ken Bell ML: Unknown BL: Unknown TR: Unknown MR: F. Dubervill BR: Ken Bell

251 TM: Ken Bell MM: Don Grant BM: S.E.E. Smith

252 TL: Unknown ML: NAC (unknown) BL: Ken Bell TR: S.E.E. Smith MR: Ernie DeGuire BR: Charlie Richer

253 TM: Charlie Richer MM: Don Grant MR: Charlie Richer BR: Ken Bell

A LAST HURRAH

A seagull
floating silently in the light breeze ...
The waves
rippling gently against the sand ...

A figure moves slowly out of the early mist.

Stopping on the beach,
he stands silent
and remembers.
Was it really so long ago?
It seems like only yesterday:
the sea-wall, the wire entanglements,
the acrid smoke
and the sounds of war with the feel of death –
then a sudden explosion and a giant blast,
the gaping crater, and a comrade gone.

He moves slowly now
beneath the rows of maple trees,
bent, searching among the countless stones.
Now, at last, erect,
beret adjusted, medals glistening,
he stands
and remembers one who did not grow old.

Slowly the hand rises in salute.
The craggy face is moist:
maybe only the soft Norman rain ...

It is indeed a last hurrah.

KEN BELL